GOT ANY
KAHLUA?

GOT ANY KAHLUA ?

The Collected Recipes of The Dude

Daniel Zwicke

First Edition
First Edition Broadway Fifth Press 2012
New York, New York
Cover Design Daniel Zwicke
First Published by Broadway Fifth Press 2012
New York, New York 2011

Library of Congress Cataloging-in-Publication Data
Zwicke, Daniel
Got Any Kahlua
ISBN-10: 1478252650
ISBN-13: 978-1478252658

1. Zwicke, Daniel, Cooks –
New York (State) --
New York, 1 Title

"A Cult gives its members license to feel superior to the rest of the Universe, and so does a Cult Movie: it confers hipness on those who get what the mainstream audiences can't."

David Edelstein,
The New York Times on The Big Lebowski

Dedicated to Fans of The Dude

and Urban Achievers Everywhere

Dude

"I'm sorry your Stepmother is a Nymphomaniac Maude."

CONTENTS

"A way out West there was this fella I want to tell you about, a fella by the name of Jeff Lebowski. At least, that was the handle his Lovin' parents gave him, but he never had much use for it himself. This Lebowski, he called himself the Dude. Now, Dude, that's a name no one would self-apply where I come from. But, then there was a whole lot about the Dude that didn't make a whole lot of sense to me. And a lot about where he lived like-wise. But then again, maybe that's why I found the place durned interesting." ....

The Cowboy Stranger

CERTAIN THINGS HAVE COME TO LIGHT

Certain Things Have Come to Light. That's right; some Very Important Things have come to light. New Shit man! What! Well The Dude and his Food for one. No the Dude doesn't only eat In-N-Out Burgers, and drink White Russians and Beer. The Dude eats other things, most people are still unaware of. And yes The Dude cooks. He has to, he's Unemployed. Ole Duder's got "Expenses" the man does not live on his good looks, smarts, and wits alone. The Dude, just like every one of us, "He Has Expenses Man." He's gotta pay Rent to *Monty* even if it is already the 10th of the Month.

The Dude has expenses. He's got Bowling Fees to pay, he's gotta buy Kahlua and quarts of ½ & 1/2, even if it is with Whale Motif Checks that Dude makes out to Ralph's. Hey Dude has his Ralph's card, so he can write them checks even if that Fascist Sheriff of Malibu does not approve . Dudes got expenses, and the only way The Dude can pay for all his necessities and needs is by stretching that limited unemployment check as far as it will possibly go. Ole "Betsy" breaks down and the Dude has to get her fixed. He's gotta buy Gas for the car and his dealer won't except his Whale Motif Check to procure the Weed. The Dude has to pay, Cold Hard Cash for that. Dude's got expenses man.

So how does our friend the Dude pay for everything? Well the Dude has got to eat. That's another expense, and though The Dude loves his In-N-Out Burgers, stops at The Taco Stands, and orders-in Chinese every now and then, with the Dudes limited amount of Funds, the Dude can't always eat out or order in. In-N-Out Burgers are not expensive, nor Chinese Take-Out, but if eaten every day, they would be. So for the unemployment checks to last and buy as much as possible, The Dude needs to "Cook Most of His Meals."

What's that you say, "You didn't know The Dude Cooks," that he knows how to cook. The Dude has to cook, he's gotta make "Each-And-Every-Dollar" he has "Stretch" as far as it will go, buy as much as he can, and he's not gonna do it by eating breakfast out, eating In-N-Out Burgers and Chinese Take Out every day. Dudes gotta cook, it's a lot Cheaper, and besides the Dude likes it, ever since his college days of Smoking A Lot of "Thai Stick" and "occupying various administration buildings." The Dude likes to cook. Like meditating and doing Tai Chi, cooking soothes the Dude's mind.

Yes The Dude likes to cook. He loves it in fact, along with bowling, driving around, "Doing-a-Little-of-This-a-Little-of-That" listening to Creedence and smoking weed, the Dude loves to cook, and he's compiled a nice collection of recipes over the years. Recipes from his Polish Granny, friends, ones he clipped out of magazines, and a few that The Dude invented and created himself. The Port Horon Statement and the yet to be seen Little Lebowski are not the only things The Dude has created over the years. He has created dishes and refined recipes that are written down in El Duderino's little wire-bound notebook. The Dude has shown me his collection of recipes and wants to share it with me, "You," The World.

Dude digs me, my great love of food, eating, my years of professional cooking experience, Travelin The World, and my Philosophy on Food, Cooking and

Eating, and how to put cooking in a simple and easy way for just about everyone to do and understand, especially all you "Achievers" out there. You gotta Eat too, "Gotta Feed the Monkey." And The Dude wants to help you with his wonderful collection of Easy to Make Recipes, recipes that will Save You Tons of Money, are not complicated (they're as Simple as can be), they don't take a lot of time to make, and Best of all, besides being economical dishes, they're as "Tasty as Can Be."

So my friends, Achievers, & all who Love and follow The Dude and all this wonderful man does, here are The Collected Recipes of The Dude. Cook, Eat, Abide!

IMPORTANT NOTE: One quick note before you go on. Being a cookbook and collection of recipes, it is not totally necessary that you read this book cover-to-cover, though we wish you would. You can hop around from recipe to recipe, Story-to-Story. However, we recommend that you do read the book cover-to-cover at least once in order to get all of the Dudes wonderful *"Duderly Advice"* and all the *information* and "Shit" that has *"Come to Light."* Then after you've read the book through once, 2, 3, or 4 times, use the book as your favorite reference to "The Dude and his Food," Year-in-and-Year-Out. Cook The Dudes Chili and Gooey Chop-Meat. Make Dude-Style Tacos, Burgers, and Burritos along with the perfect Dude instructed White Russian, "Enjoy and Abide!"

GOT ANY KAHLUA ?

Kahlua is a Mexican Coffee Flavored Liqueur that is Rum based. Kahlua has a distinct Coffee taste, it's sweet tasty and thick on the tongue. Kahlua also contains; Sugar and Vanilla Bean. Kahlua is 20% alcohol.

Kahlua was first created in 1936 by Pedro Domecq in Veracruz, Mexico. Kahlua means "The House of The Acolhua" people of Pre-Spanish Veracruz, Mexico.

Kahlua is used to make various cocktails and as a topping for many deserts, which include; Ice Cream, Cakes, Chocolates, and Cheesecake.

Some of the most popular Cocktails that Kahlua is used as a primary ingredient are; The B52, Black Russian, Mudslide, The "Blow Job" Bunny Lebowski's favorite for "Obvious Reason," the Blow Job is made of Bailey's Irish Cream with Kahlua and topped with Whipped Cream. How cum so much Cream Bunny? Another favorite Bunny Lebowski Cock-Tail based on Kahlua is of course the "Orgasm," made with Kahlua, Amaretto, ½ & ½, and Bailey's on the Rocks. And of course thee All-Time # 1 Kahlua based Cocktail "The Dudes" beloved White Russian, or as the Dude calls them, Caucasians, Caucasian singular.

It is believed that the Dude first discovered and became enamored with Kahlua and his beloved White Russian sometime in the 70's and has been drinking them ever since. "Fuckin Eh!"

THE CAUCASIAN
a.k.a. WHITE RUSSIAN

"Careful Man, I've got a beverage here!"

The White Russian, the beloved drink of our hero, "The Dude." He just loves them, and as he calls them "Caucasians" or a Caucasian. The Stranger likes himself Sarsaparilla, Sioux City Sarsaparilla to be exact. Walter likes his Beer, so does Donny, and the Dude likes Beer too, but nowhere as much as his cherished Caucasian.

The Caucasian or as most other people call them, the White Russian is a drink that is a spin-off of an older drink, the Black Russian, made of Vodka and Coffee Liquor (Kahlua or Tia Maria) over ice in an Old-Fashion or Rocks Glass. The Black Russian was invented in 1949. There seems to be no exact data on when The Dudes beloved White Russian was invented and first served. It's been recognized that one of the first print documentations of the White Russian Cocktail was in The Oakland Tribune in November of 1965. It has also been said that even before this, there was an ad for Southern Comfort in the Boston Globe that predates this 1965 publication of which a White Russian Cocktail was in the advertisement. Don't know why. This ad was sometime in the first half of the 1960's decade, but an exact date is nowhere to be found. So here we have, The White Russian being born sometime in the early 1960's.

Now boys and Girls, have you ever wondered why The Dude of all people drinks a White Russian

(Caucasian), a drink considered to be a "Girly Drink" ? Well, I can tell you why. The Dude likes them, his beloved Caucasian. He likes the way they taste and he doesn't "Give a F_ck" that it's a Girly Drink aka P_ssy Drink. The Dude doesn't give a Sh_t who likes it or not, or if anyone looks at him strangely for drinking one. The Dude is eccentric. He's not a follower, The Dude dances to the beat of his own drum, "Fuckin Eh."

So there you have it my fellow Achievers, a brief little history and background on The Dudes much loved "Caucasian" The White Russian Cocktail," make it, it drink, and Abide!

Stranger: *"I Dig Your Style DUDE, but do you have to Cuss so much?" (as he sips Sarsaparilla)*

Dude: *"What The FUCK are you talking about?!" (as he sips a White Russian)*

Stranger: *"OK, have er your way Dude."*

"I'll HAVE ANOTHER CAUCASIAN GARY"

The White Russian Cocktail as we've so far learned is a Spin-Off of the Black Russian, created in 1949. The White Russian (Caucasian as per The Dude) was born sometime in the early 1960's. Like practically all cocktail recipes, none are always exact. There are different ratios of the liquor and other ingredients such as juices, soda, bitters, and in this case of the White Russian, Milk, Cream, or Half-And-Half. The ingredients for a White Russian are: Vodka, Coffee Liqueur (Kahlua preferred, or Tia Maria or other brand). Many recipes for the cocktail call for equal parts of each; Vodka, Coffee Liqueur, and Milk or Cream, about 1 ounce of each in an Old-Fashion or Rocks Glass filled with ice cubes the Milk or Cream, Vodka, and Kahlua. Some recipes call for 1 oz. Vodka, 1 ½ oz. Kahlua and topped with Milk or Cream. This is the Way The Dude likes his, with a bit more of his cherished Kahlua and a little less Vodka, and the Dude prefers half & half, though in a pinch he'll use milk or non-dairy creamer as he was forced to do when making a "Caucasian" at Maude's house. So, for all you Achievers out there who want to drink their "Caucasians" just like The Dudes, there you go. The Dude always uses Kahlua, never Tia Maria or any other brands, but in a pinch, if you want to, go right ahead. The Dude always prefers his Caucasians with Half & Half but will use milk or other when the half-and-half is not available.

WHITE RUSSIAN
a.k.a. "CAUCASIAN"

1 ½ ounces Kahlua or other Coffee Liquor
1 oz. Vodka
Half & Half (or whole Milk)
Ice Cubes

1. Fill an Old-Fashion or Rocks Glass with ice.

2. Pour in Vodka. Pour in Kahlua, and then top with Half & Half to just below rim.

3. Stir. It's ready. Abide and Enjoy.

Notes: As stated early, you can make a White Russian with 1 oz. each equal parts Kahlua, Vodka, and Milk, Cream, or half & half. You can put in a little more vodka than the coffee liquor and vice-versa. The above recipe is the way The Dude likes his White Russians made with a bit more of The Dude's treasured Kahlua than Vodka.

PS .. Dudes preferred Vodka is Smirnoff, a great old school Vodka that is just good and not overpriced due to expensive advertising and marketing. Dude also likes Gordon's, and also Popov, and Wolfsmidt's which are both very good quality lower priced Vodka's. Dude would never ever use the grossly "Overpriced and Over-Rated" brands like Chopin, Belvedere, Grey Goose and other similar Vodka's. Dude says that they are no better than his Smirnoff's and people who buy them are fools. Dude says, "Don't get caught in their marketing trap." Abide with Gordon's, Smirnoff, Popov, or Wolfsmidt's.

BUNNY'S BJ COCK-TAIL
"I'll Suck Your Co_k for a Thousand Dollars"

RECIPE:
½ ounce KAHLUA
½ ounce Bailey's Irish Cream
Whipped Cream (fresh or from a Can is fine)

Place the Kahlua in a shot glass. Add Bailey's.
Top with Whipped Cream and Enjoy!
This Bunny's Favorite Cocktail for obvious reasons.
She loves the preferred and recommended way to drink
it (Swallow It) proper.

Proper way to drink a BJ is put your mouth around
it, like it's a "you know what," then Suck It Down in
one full swoop.
"But Brandt can't watch or he has to pay $100 ..
And "Yes" the name of this Cocktail is a "Blowjob."
It's has been around since the late 70's.

"GOTTA FEED THE MONKEY" !!!

A "ZESTY"
"and a Zesty Enterprise it is"

Yes a Zesty Enterprise it is, The Zesty, Maude's favorite Cocktail made with Prosecco on Ice with a splash of Campari, a dash of club soda, garnished with a nice juicy slice of Orange. Maude discovered the "Zesty" in Italy, while showing her "Strongly Vaginal Art" at the Venice Biennale with Sandra and Knox Harrington the Video Artist. They are from Venice and are really called *Spritz*. Maude changed the name, for her own little thing. Yes it's a Zesty Enterprise Maudy, but Dude says, "leave your friend Knox with the Cleft Asshole at home."

THE ZESTY

4 ounces Prosecco
½ oz. Campari or Aperol
2 oz. Club Soda or Sparkling Mineral Water
½ an Orange slice
Ice Cubes

The Zesty is best served in a long stem balloon wine glass, and can also be served in a High-Ball, Collins, or Rock Glass.
Fill glass with Ice. Add Prosecco, then Campari. Add Club Soda. Garnish with Orange slice.
Maude: Do you like Sex Mr. Lebowski?

Dude: Excuse Me?

Got Any Kahlua?

Maude: Sex. The physical act of love. Coitus. Do you like it?

Dude: I was talking about my rug.

Maude: You're not interested in Sex?

Dude: You mean Coitus?

Maude: I like it too. It's a male myth about feminists that we hate sex. It can be a natural, zesty enterprise. However there are some people--it is called satyriasis in men, nymphomania in women--who engage in it compulsively and without joy.

Dude: Oh No!

Maude: Oh yes Mr. Lebowski, these unfortunate souls cannot love in the true sense of the word. Our mutual acquaintance Bunny is one of these.

Dude: Listen, Maude uh, I'm sorry if your *Stepmother* is a *Nympho*, but uh, I don't see what this has to do with uh--do you have any KAHLUA?

BUNNY LEBOWSKI'S
PORNO PUNCH

Besides Blow Job Cock-tails, Bunny Lebowski drinks these tasty beverages while lounging out at The Pool and in-between doing things for a Thousand-Dollars, "But Brandt Can't Watch" or he has to pay a Hundred

The Houseboy who carried "The Rug" out to The Dudes car prepares and serves these for Bunny, or as Walter likes to call her "That Slut."

1 ½ ounce Light Rum
1 ounce Dark Rum
1/4 oz. Triple Sec, Cointreau, or Grand Marnier
3 dashes of Angostura Bitters
Splash of Grenadine or Cherry Liquor
3 oz. Orange Juice (Fresh Squeezed Preferred)
2 oz. Pineapple Juice

1. Fill a cocktail shaker with ice.

2. Add all the ingredients. Shake and pour into a balloon wine glass or some kind of tall glass. Garnish with either a slice of orange, lemon, lime, or Pineapple.

Drink and Enjoy, and don't do anything The Dude wouldn't do.

The Big Lebowski: *Are you employed Sir?*

Dude: Employed?

Got Any Kahlua?

The Big Lebowski: *You don't go out looking for a job dressed like that. On a weekday?*

Dude: *Is this a .... What day is this?*

The Big Lebowski: *Well, I do work Sir, so if you don't mind ...*

Dude: *I do mind, the Dude minds. This will not stand, ya know, This aggression will not stand Man!*

DUDE'S KAHLUA SPIKED FRUIT SHAKES

Ingredients:

2 whole fresh Bananas
1 12 oz. can Sliced Peaches (drain syrup off)
1 cup whole Milk
3 ounces Kahlua
4 large Ice Cubes

Place all ingredients in blender container. Blend for 2-3 minutes, pour in your favorite glass and Enjoy.

Some days The Dude likes to start his mornings off with a glass or 2 of this refreshing and somewhat healthy beverage. It's either one or two of these or a coffee and a glass of The Kahlua spiked Fruit Shake.

You can change up the ingredients to make variations on this basic recipe. Dude sometimes subs fresh Strawberries for the peaches; he sometimes throws in a couple tablespoons of Peanut Butter, and a scoop or two of Vanilla or Chocolate Ice Cream whenever he has some on hand. Drink and Abide !

Dude: *She probably Kidnapped herself.*

Donny: *What do you mean Dude?*

Dude: *Rug Pee-ers did not do this. Look at it. A young trophy wife, marries this guy for his money, she figures he hasn't given her enough, she owes money all over town.*

Walter: *That Fucking Bitch !!!*

THE DUDE and FOOD
"and HOW to USE THIS BOOK"

The Dude and Food? Yes the Dude likes his food. Actually, along with Bowling, getting "High," imbibing in his favorite drink The White Russians, driving around, listening to Creedence, Tai Chi, and "A Little Bit of This a Little Bit of That," food, cooking, and eating is a major part of The Dudes life, when he's not getting mixed up in faux kidnappings and acting as courier, Bowling, or having a coffee at the coffee shop with Walter, discussing life, the World, philosophizing, or what not, "What about The Fucking Toe" ??? The Dude likes to cook.

The Dude has amassed quite a nice collection of recipes over the years. He learned how to cook Home Fries from his dad who gave the little Dude some early wisdom when he told his little Jeffrey, "Son every man needs to know how to cook a few good dishes. You gotta be able to cook yourself some Eggs and Potatoes for Breakfast, how to work the barbecue grill and how to cook a Proper Steak." Dudes mom and granny showed The Young Dude a thing or two as well. Dude got a few recipes from friends after being at parties or what not, liking a particular dish (like Burritos, Tacos, and what not) and asking the host or whoever made the dish for the recipe. Dude clipped out some recipes from newspapers and food, home, and garden, magazines, and got a bunch of books at garages sales and Flea Markets, just a Quarter a Pop. He scoured through these

16

and came up with a number of good dishes he uses all the time.

The Dude has a spiral note-book where he has written down recipes or taped in clipped recipes from magazines and newspapers. It's an interesting collection, and gives us a little bit more insight into The Dude, his likes and dislikes.

This collection of The Dudes Recipes, info, and advice on food, and cooking, Life too, and a little bit of Duder philosophy here and there.

This collection of Dudes Recipes, a cookbook, is not set up and written in the normal order that you see most cookbooks written, with appetizers, to start out, then maybe a chapter on soup, followed by main course dishes with fish dishes and recipes leading the way, followed by poultry, then meat, and the cookbook ends with deserts.

The Dude's Collected Recipes starts out with the most important things first and goes in order of importance with The White Russian being most important and thus the first recipe. There is a handful of Cocktail Recipes and wisdom, then we go into food, starting with some of Dudes favorite, most eaten recipes, like Eggs, Tuna, Chili and related recipes, soups, and on down the line.

Dude wants you to learn first-things-first. Get a handful of recipes and knowledge, build on these, and then learn one or two other things (Dishes), "Taken Her Easy" as the Cowboy Stranger would say. For example, Dude starts out with some basics on cooking Eggs, which are very easy, super quick to prepare, "Tasty," and cheap too. All major requirements for The Dude, his food, cooking, and the recipes he likes.

So you start out slow, learn the basics, going step-by-step and building on what you learn. A beginning foundation, learn the inexpensive, easy, nutritious Home Fries, how to make Hard Boiled Eggs, and how to Fry an Egg and you're off to a nice little start. You learn the home fries, fried and scrambled eggs and you can make yourself a plate of potatoes and eggs for breakfast or any time. And once you know how to make yourself some good scrambled eggs and Fried Eggs, then you'll be able to make a good number of different and varied Egg Sandwiches, like; Ham and Egg, Fried Egg and Cheese, or Ham Egg and Cheese, whatever. Nothing like a "Tasty" quick and easy Egg Sandwich, they're not just for breakfast, they make a great lunch, late night snack after Bowling, or anytime of the day, they're great, and good to know how to make.

When you know how to make hard Boiled Eggs, which is the easiest thing in the world, you can eat them as is or make the laughably simple Egg Salad for tasty and *zesty* little Egg Salad Sandwiches anytime of the day. Again; quick, easy, tasty, and inexpensive. The Dude likes them, so does Maude, or Maudy, as Knox would say.

Right after learning about Eggs, you'll learn about Tuna, canned Tuna, not the fresh stuff. The Dude likes his food fresh, especially fruits and vegetables, all his fish, except of course Tuna, which he likes canned man. Yes he likes everything fresh, with two exceptions, Iced Tea and "Tuna." When it comes to tuna, it's gotta be canned. And a can of Tuna for The Dude is a longtime old true and tried *friend,* ever since Dudes College Days and helping to author the Port Horon Statement.

Yes The Dude subsisted and lived on canned Tuna, Spaghetti, and the occasional Burger, and leftover pizza. Dude is quite individualistic, and totally unique, but when it came to college days of smoking a lot of Thai Stick and occupying various administration buildings, in these days, the Dudes-Food and eating habits were much like most college age American males, Burgers, Pizza, and canned Tuna. Canned Tuna, a.k.a. a single guys *best-friend*, and that includes our hero, The Dude.

Make the Dudes Classic Tuna Salad recipe and the wonderful and satisfying Macaroni & Tuna Salad. It's awesome and especially refreshing thing to eat during hot summer months, and super economical too.

After the Tuna, you'll move on to one of the Dudes most beloved and quite versatile food items, in Chili. Chili and all the things you can do with it, like; Chili con Carne, 3-Way Chili, Beef Burritos or Tacos stuffed with Dudes Chili. These are Dudes favorites of all, Tacos and Burritos made with his Chili and a few other ingredients thrown into the assemblage.

Once Dude has his Chili, he just serves it in a bowl with all the necessary condiments, like chopped onions, shredded Cheese, and crackers. And The Dude usually grabs himself a nice cold Beer when sitting down to enjoy a bowl of his specially made Cowboy Chili. Yumm!!!!

That's just like your opinion Man!"

The DUDE

JESUS: "Don't F_ck with The Jesus Mannn!"

DONNY: "JEEZE"

JESUS: "You Said It Mannn!"

DUDES BREAKFAST
and EGGS

Dude, he really loves himself a nice hearty Breakfast and Dude knows and Abides, that Breakfast is the most important meal of the day. Dude sometimes has Cereal (Cheerios and Captain Crunch are his favorites), French Toast, or even some Lingonberry Pancakes from a recipe that Walter beat out of the Nihilist. But most of all, Dude likes a nice plate of Scrambled or Fried Eggs with Home Fries made from his dads famed home fries recipe.

Yes, The Dude most days, brews up a pot of coffee, puts on some Creedence and starts cooking the potatoes. When the home fries are almost done, The Dude fries up a couple eggs, then sits down with yesterday's paper, his cup of Joe and the plate of tasty Home Fries and Eggs, and the Dude starts off his day satiated, happy, and well informed, even if it is yesterday's news, naturally recycled by The Dude.

Yes, the Dude loves his eggs, they are quick and easy to make. They are tasty and cheap and the Dude realizes something, it's crazy most Americans don't know, Eggs are not just for breakfast. Eggs are great, any time of the day, yes breakfast, lunch, dinner, late night and any time in-between.

Dude eats eggs all the time, especially one of his renowned Egg Sandwiches like a Fried Egg and Cheese Sandwich or Dudes faves, Taylor Ham or Spam & Egg Sandwiches. Yumm, the Dude just loves them, and eats them often after a night of bowling with the boys, Walter and Donny.

Did you know? Breakfast used to be a lot cheaper in diners and the Dude liked that. Unfortunately, you can't get 2 eggs with home fries, coffee, and toast for $2.99 plus a dollar tip for about $4.25 with tax. Nowadays this breakfast will set back almost twice that, or about $7.00 and if you want Ham or sausages on the plate, that breakfast is gonna set you back 9 or 10 Dollars. Not a lot of money but multiply that by the 300 plus times a year that the Dude cooks breakfast at home and you're talking about $2,700. A cup of coffee, 2 eggs and home fries cost Dude about .75 cents to make at home, for a net gain of an average of $6.00 a breakfast. Sometimes Dude goes to the deli and gets a breakfast special of a coffee and buttered roll, a bagel and coffee, or coffee and ham & Egg Sandwich for about $3.00, but Dude likes to cook breakfast, most days, just not always.

On weekend mornings, The Dude sometimes likes to throw on some nice soothing Classical Music, like Vivaldi or Mozart on and whip up some coffee, French Toast, or Pancakes, sit down eating his breakfast to the soothing relaxing classical tunes is just fine. Then he'll do a little Tai Chi, and it's on to another day.

And, by the way, Dude has estimated that he saves about $1,500 a year by eating and cooking breakfast at home. And this doesn't include all the money he saves cooking lunch and dinner, which amounts to about $6,000 a year. Wow, that's a lot of Kahlua!

DUDES DAD'S HOME-FRIES

Yes Dude's Dad as we've already said, always cooked Breakfast Saturday mornings in the Lebowski house-hold. He was renowned for these Home-Fries. Here's how you make them. And keep in mind these home fries are not just for breakfast with eggs, you can serve them alongside and meat, poultry or fish dish you make, with Steak, Pork Chops, Chicken, Whatever.

INGERDIENTS: For four people.

Cut recipe in half for 1 or two
4 Idaho, Maine, or Russet Potatoes
4 tablespoons Vegetable or Olive Oil
Salt & Ground Black Pepper to taste
½ teaspoon Sweet Paprika

1. Place potatoes in water to cover. Add 1 tablespoon of salt. Bring to boil. Let Potatoes boil for 30 seconds. Drain the Potatoes in a colander.

2. Heat oil over medium flame for 1 minute. Add the potatoes to oil. Season potatoes with, Paprika and Salt & Pepper to taste. Cook over medium heat for about 10 to 12 minutes stirring the Potatoes from time to time with a wooden spoon.

3. The Home Fries are ready to serve with eggs.

NOTE: You can add 1 medium diced or sliced onion for a little more taste. You would add the onions after the potatoes have been cooking for five minutes. You can also add some sliced Mushrooms with the onion and even some frozen Peas. Experiment and enjoy.

Dude: *"Nobody calls me Lebowski!*
I'm The Dude!"

Treehorn Thug # 1: *"You're Lebowski,*
Lebowski. Your wife is Bunny."

Dude: *"My Wife? Do I look like I'm Fucking*
Married? The Fucking Toilet-Seat
is up Man!"

EGGS "DUDES WAY"

So, you have cooked The Dude's Dad's Home Fries and you've got that down pat. Give yourself a pat on the back. This is a great start. The home fires are cheap, easy, and tasty. They fill you up and can be served alongside anything. Almost! Now, Dude says you gotta know your "Basic on Eggs," they will serve you well. Hard Boiled Eggs are the easiest thing in the World to learn how to make. Just as easy as Tuna-Fish, and they are both quite versatile. You got some Hard Boiled Eggs, you peel them, sprinkle on some salt & pepper, perhaps a dollop of mayo, pop em in your mouth.

You can make some Egg Salad, always great to have on hand to make Egg Salad Sandwiches any time you might get the urge. Make one and bring it to The Bowling Alley. Soaks up the Beer real good, White Russians too.

You got yourself some egg salad on hand, it makes a nice element to many a composed salad. Pack yourself 2 or 3 hard Boiled Eggs and a Banana or two when on a road trip and you've always got something on hand if you get hungry. Healthy too. The Dude knows what he's doing man!

So eggs? Versatile little suckers they are. You gotta learn how to Fry them, Scramble them, soft or hard boil them, and don't forget they'll serve you well.

"What About The FUCKING TOE ?"

Dude

"You Want a Toe Dude? I can get you a Toe. I can get you one by 3 o'clock, and with nail polish. You don't wanna know."

"Fucking amateurs! They send us a Toe and expect us to Shit our Pants in fear. Fucking amateurs."

Walter Sobchak

SOFT BOILED

Did you know that they have Special little holders just for Soft Boiled Eggs that are really nice and can be quite *elegant* or *whimsical* if you wish.

When I was a young child I used to Love eating Soft Boiled Eggs from the Little Clown Egg Holder that my mother bought for me. Wish I still had that! I Loved it. Dude said he had one of those buggers too. He still has his and goes back to his childhood whenever he pops in some toast as he's cooking his soft-boiler. Four minutes and she's done. Dude got his cup of coffee, and he butters some toast, then places the Soft Boiled Egg in his Clown Soft Boiled Egg Holder. Cool man! He cracks into the top of the egg. Scoops some out and onto the toast. Takes a sip of coffee. Yumm, just the way The Dude likes things, simple, uncomplicated, and easy. And when it comes to food, tasty and cheap will do The Dude just fine, "Thank You."

If you don't have one of these special egg-holder like the Dude, don't fret. Serve the eggs on a regular plate with buttered toast and enjoy. The Clown Egg Holder does make the experience a bit more fun. Quite animated, especially for kids, and the Dude wouldn't eat them any other way.

COOKING THE SOFT-BOILED EGG

1. Take an Egg, 1, 2, 3, or for, however many you need. Usually when eating Soft Boiled Eggs, people have just one with one or two Pieces of Butter Toast.

2. OK, you get an Egg; One, Two, Three, or Four. Put the Egg or Eggs in a small pot and cover the eggs with water.

3. Turn the heat to high and bring water to the boil. As soon as the water comes to the boil, lower the heat so the water is at a slow simmer. Time 4 minutes from this point, and let the Eggs cook in the lightly simmering water for 4 minutes for a Four-Minute-Egg or 3 minutes for a 3 Minute Egg which will naturally be cooked less. For me and most people a Four Minute Egg is best.

4. Remove the egg from the water and put it in a Special Soft Boiled Egg Cup (Holder)

5. Oh! I almost forgot. How to eat the Egg? Just in case you don't know. Simply take a teaspoon and crack the egg in a circle going around the top of the egg. Take off the top of the egg. Scoop the egg out of the shell and place on toast. Eat and Enjoy, and always Abide!

HARD BOILED
"NOT THE PERSON.. THE EGG"

The Hard Boiled Egg? Simplest thing you could ever make in your life. In fact it's so simple that it's used in an expression for terrible cooks. The saying is, "He's so bad (about their cooking), he couldn't boil an Egg." Can say this about The Dude, though I bet lots of people would have thought you could.

1. Follow steps one to three of a Soft Boiled Egg.

2. Put the eggs in water, bring to boil, then lower to a simmer, and time from this point, 8 minutes. In 8 minutes of the egg cooking in low simmering water, you will have a Hard Boiled Egg that is solid throughout. It does not have a soft runny yolk in the center like a Soft Boiled Egg.

3. The other big difference in a Soft Boiled and Hard Boiled Eggs are that you eat Soft Boiled Eggs hot and hard Boiled Eggs Cold. So, once your eggs have cooked for 8 minutes. Remove them from the heat. Drain the hot water off. Place the pot with the eggs in a sink and run cold water over the eggs for several minutes to cool them. Let the eggs cool down, and then drain turn cold water off. Put hard boiled eggs in refrigerator to get cold and they will be ready to make Egg Salad, Nicoise or Cobb Salad. You're set.

"The Dude Abides. I don't know about you but I take comfort in that. It's good knowin' he's out there. The Dude. Takin' 'er easy for all us sinners. Shoosh I sure hopes he makes the finals."

Cowboy Stranger

FRIED EGGS

Fried Eggs along with Scrambled are the most popular to eat for Breakfast and are absolutely great for lunch or a light meal any time of the day. They are very easy to make, though people have been known to screw them up. Not The Dude. And The Dude knows one of the most important things to remember is to have a hot pan and use a non-stick one for best and easiest results. The Eggs will slide right outa the pan. No sticking here.

Get proficient and learn and teach yourself along with The Dudes recipe and guidance, how to Fry Up a good Egg. With a Fried Egg and Dudes Home Fries you got a right nice breakfast right there. Make a fried egg or two, and cook up some ramen, serve the ramen dry coated with some Sesame Oil and a bit of Hot Sauce and you've got yourself a quick meal in less than 10 minutes. Cheap too. About .55 cents a plate. Now you have more money for Kahlua, Bowling, and other essentials.

Got a fried Egg and you make any number of variations of a Fried Egg Sandwich in 5 minutes time. Taylor Ham and Egg, Spam and Egg, or a Egg and Cheese Sandwich, lickity-split. You know Dude likes that, any time of day.

HOW to MAKE A FRIED EGG

1. Heat a Non-Stick Pan over medium heat for 3 minutes. Add vegetable oil and heat for 3 minutes until hot. You want the eggs to start cooking the second they

hit the pan. If the oil is not hot enough the eggs won't start cooking immediately and your results won't be as good.

2. Once your oil is hot enough, place two eggs in pan with hot oil. Cook for 1 ½ to 3 minutes for a Sunny Side Up Egg. Season eggs with Salt & Black Pepper.

3. If you want Eggs Over Easy, after cooking the eggs for 2 ½ to 3 minutes on the first side, you'll flip the eggs over and cook for about 30 seconds on the second side.

4. Remove the eggs from the pan and serve.

5. For Eggs Over Hard, you will cook the eggs for 1 - ½ to 2 minutes on the second side, then serve.

SCRAMBLED

As we've stated earlier, Scrambled Eggs are the most popular way to eat Eggs for Breakfast in the United States. As with the Fried Eggs, Scrambled Eggs make a nice light meal that is a good and inexpensive source of protein any time of the day. Dude makes some Home Fries and grabs the bottle of Catsup (Ketchup) which goes great with the fries and scramble. And of course, just like the fried egg, scramble eggs go on any Egg Sandwich, and they're great with Ramen.

1. Take two or three eggs and crack them into a small bowl. Discard shells. Season eggs with salt and pepper. Beat eggs with a fork for one minute.

2. Heat a small Non-Stick Frying Pan over medium heat for 2 minutes. Add 2 tablespoons of oil. Heat for two minutes. When the oil has heated, add 1 teaspoon of butter to pan and let melt.

3. As soon as the butter has melted, turn heat up to high and quickly add the beaten eggs to pan. Cook for 1 minute over high heat stirring eggs with a wooden spoon or rubber spatula.

4. Turn heat down to medium flame and continue stirring and cooking eggs until they are cooked through and there is not raw egg.

5. Remove eggs from pan and put on a plate with Home Fries and Ham or Breakfast Sausage if you like. For a little more flavor you can a little bit of butter over the eggs once they are on the plate and still hot. Also

sprinkle Salt & Black Pepper over eggs at this time and you can also put on some Hot Sauce and or Ketchup if you choose to do so or not. "Enjoy!"

OMELETS DUDES WAY

Omelets? What are they? Well they can be anything. "Filled" with anything that is. More or less, an Omelet is eggs that are beaten, seasoned with salt and pepper and cooked in a pan with butter much like Scrambled Eggs. The difference being in that Scrambled Eggs are broken up into pieces of cooked egg and an omelets is cooked and left in one whole mass of eggs and in which the Omelet is filled with some sort of filling like; Sautéed Mushrooms, Bacon, Cheese, vegetables and a multitude of ingredients whereby the omelet takes on the name of the filling ingredients, such as a Bacon Cheddar Omelet or a Mushroom Omelets, but the possibilities of the ingredient so put inside an omelet is almost endless, and The Dude likes that. If he's got some leftover stir-fried vegetables from the not before, guess what, Dudes throwing them in his Omelet he makes for lunch the next day and The Dudes got himself a nice Stir-Fried Veg Omelet. Yumm! But even better than that is The Dudes "Famous" Chili Cheese Omelet. They're renowned in Dudeville. Walter gobbles them up like they're going out of style, Donny "God Rest his Soul" loved them, and Dudes been able to butter Monte up into letting him send in the rent as late as the 20th because of The Dudes thoughtfulness in whipping-up one of his Famed Chili Cheese Omelets and bring it over to Montes place. No sweat on The Dude, it gave him another 10 days to get the rent money together. Maybe it can help you too. No matter, the tastiness and enjoyment of these little babies is more than enough, even if you're unable to persuade your landlord the way Dude has done with Monte.

When it comes to Omelet's they are most famous in Classical French Cuisine, though, not percentagewise but on a whole, more omelets are eaten in the United States than anywhere else in the World, but guess where they were invented? In the Middle East.

In France the most popular Omelets are; Mushroom, Goat Cheese, and Fine Herbs (mixed fresh herbs) while in the United States you'll find Bacon & Cheddar, Mushrooms, Ham & Cheese, or the Denver Omelet are most popular. All this being said, in the past few years the Italian Omelet, the Frittata is gaining ground in the U.S. little by little and for me, being Italian-American, the Frittata is my personal favorite. They are the most practical and useful. The Frittata (Italian Omelet) is a flat omelet that takes the shape of the pan and can be filled with an endless variety of ingredients. My favorite Frittati are Spaghetti and Sausage and Pepper.

One of the great things with the Italian Style omelet is that it can be served cold or at room temperature as well as hot out of the pan. Also Frittata can be cut into wedges; and can be served as Antipasto, as a snack out of the frig any time of the day, at picnics, or to take along in the car on a long road trip. Much more versatile than any other omelet that needs to be eaten on the spot.

Back to the Denver Omelet. It has a great name, and that's probably why Quentin Tarrantino used it in a scene in the masterpiece Pulp Fiction when Tim Roth prior to sticking up a Diner he is eating at with his girlfriend Honey-Bunny (no relation to Bunny Lebowski) tells her how easy it will be to rob a Diner. He points out that some "Poor F_ _k" is eating his

Denver Omelet and the next thing he knows he's got a F_ _kin Gun pointed in his face, Never expecting this to happen.

So, try to learn these things, how to make an omelet if you can, The Dude says. They are a bit harder to learn than just making scrambled or fried eggs. Takes a little practice, but it doesn't cost you much. Dude says, practice making them just when you at home cooking for yourself and not for company. You'll catch on soon enough. And Dude says, you can really impress the ladies if you make an Omelet in the morning for "That Special Lady Friend," and you don't have to "Help Her to Conceive." Not if you don't want to. Maude, you sly little Devil, "Devilette."

So Dude says, don't let these things intimidate you, practice up, and if you want to skip them, Dude says it's OK, only problem being, you won't be able to make the Dudes "Famous Chili Cheese Omelet." Don't fret, you can always just mix in some of Dude's Chili into some scrambled eggs and top them

with Cheddar or Monterey Jack Cheese. They won't look quite the same as a Dude Chili Cheese Omelet, but they'll taste just as good, and ole Duder is OK with that.

Note: Omelet is spelled a couple different ways. It can be spelled with 1 or 2 "t," as; Omelet or Omelette, either way is correct.

The DENVER OMELET

"One minute you're eating a Denver Omelet, the next minute you gotta a Fu_king Gun in your face!"

Tim Roth at Diner in PULP FICTION

RECIPE

2 (or 3) Extra Large or Jumbo
1/3 cup of Sliced Mushrooms
1 slice of ham cut into strips (Julienne)
¼ cup of a Red and or Green Bell Pepper diced
2 teaspoons of vegetable oil (Canola, Corn, etc.)
Salt and Ground Black Pepper
1 Scallion (Green Onion) sliced

1. Place a small Non-Stick Frying Pan over a burner on the stove top and turn the heat on to a medium flame. Add oil and let heat 2 minutes. Add green peppers and cook for three minutes, stirring occasionally.

2. Add Mushrooms and cook for 3 minutes. Add Scallions. Cook for 3 minutes.
3. Crack the eggs into a small bowl. Season with salt and pepper. Beat the eggs until they are one solid color of yellow.

4. Add ham to pan and cook for 1 minute.
5. Remove contents of pan to a plate or bowl on the side. Turn heat up to high. Add butter.

6. Heat butter for 30 seconds, then add the Beaten Eggs to pan. Cook eggs while stirring just a little bit for one minute.

7. Lower flame to medium and let eggs cook through and form one whole round mass the same shape as the pan.

8. Turn heat off. Place the reserved ham and vegetables over one side of the eggs. Fold the other side of eggs over the vegetables.

9. Place your Denver Omelet on a plate. Eat and Enjoy and always Abide!

NOTE: Egg White Omelets are very popular these days with people looking to cut down on the high cholesterol in an egg yolk. To make an Egg White Denver Omelet, use three eggs. Break the eggs one at a time into a bowl. After you crack one egg into the bowl, you need to remove the yolk with your hand. Do the same with the remaining 2 eggs. You will end up with a bowl of three egg whites. Add salt and pepper and beat the egg whites and proceed in the same manner as you would have with the whole eggs.

DUDES "SHROOM OMELET"
"A BACON & CHEESE Too"

Using the same procedure as you would in this recipe for a Denver Omelet, you can make 100 other Omelet types simply by changing the ingredients. To make a Mushroom Omelet (*Dudes Shroom*), you would omit all the other filling ingredients of a Denver Omelet, but you would double the amount of sautéed mushrooms, and you've got yourself a nice Mushroom Omelet.

To make a Bacon & Cheddar Cheese Omelet, you would dice up two or three slices of Bacon. Cook the bacon, removing most of the Bacon Fat. You would grate or chop some good quality Cheddar Cheese, then add the Bacon and Cheddar to the middle of the cooked eggs. You've got yourself a Bacon Cheddar Cheese Omelet!

If you like omelets, you can experiment and put whatever ingredients you want into your omelet, creating your very own Omelet Creations. "You can give them whatever name you like."

Experiment, Eat, and Enjoy!

DUDE'S CHILI CHEESE OMELET

2 or 3 Extra Large Eggs
(depends how Hungry you are)
¼ cup Dudes Killer Chili, heated through
Salt & Pepper to taste
2 oz. grated Cheddar or Monterey Jack Cheese
2 tablespoons Canola, Olive, or Corn Oil
3 tablespoons chopped Scallions or Onions (Optional)

1. Heat the Chili and set aside.

2. Beat eggs in a bowl with salt & pepper.

3. Heat a small non-stick frying pan over medium heat. Place oil in pan, let heat 1 minute.

4. If using scallions or onions, add now. Cook on Medium heat for 3 minutes.

5. Add half the heated Chili. Turn heat up to high flame.

6. Add eggs and cook stirring constantly until eggs set up into one solid mass in pan.

7. Place the omelet on a plate. Add half the cheese and half the Chili on side of omelet. Fold omelet over. Place remaining Chili on top of omelet. Place remaining Cheese on top of Chili "Congrats" you've just made the famous Dude Chili Cheese Omelet. Eat, Enjoy, and Abide in this wonder-fully fabulous feat. The World is yours.

NIHILIST LINGONBERRY PANCAKES

Donny: "They were Nazis Dude?"

Dude: "No Donny, they were Nihilist. They kept saying they don't believe in anything!"

Donny: "Jeeze."

DUDE and WALTER Having a CUP of JOE

Dude: "What about the Fucking Toe" ???!!!!

Walter: "You want a toe? I can get you a TOE! Believe me, there are ways, Dude. You don't want to know about it, believe me. Hell, I can get you a Toe by 3 o'clock this afternoon, with nail polish."

Walter: "Fucking Amateurs!!! They send us a *Toe* and expect us to Shit our pants in fear!"

LINGONBERRY PANCAKES (serves 4)

1 Cup Fresh Lingonberries
1 cup Milk
½ cup All-Purpose Flour
2 large Eggs
3 tablespoons melted Butter (plus additional b

Got Any Kahlua?

Butter to cook the Pancakes in.
2 tablespoons Sugar and a Dash of Salt

1. In a medium bowl, mix Loganberries with sugar and set aside.

2. In a large bowl mix flour and milk and whisk with a wire-whisk until smooth. Add eggs, butter, & salt and mix until smooth.

3. Heat a non-stick pan or non-stick electric griddle to medium heat. Coat pan (griddle) with melted butter.

4. Add enough batter to pan to make desired size pancake. Cook about 2 minutes until pancake starts to bubble. Flip pancake to other side with a rubber spatula. Cook until pancake is slightly golden brown. Continue making pancakes until
all the pancake batter is used up.

5. Serve Pancakes 2 or 3 per person. Put a portion of Lingonberries on each plate.

NOTE: If you have whipped cream and want to serve it with the pancakes that's great. You can sprinkle the pancakes with confectionary 10X sugar, or simple serve just with the Lingonberries.

PS … Dude says, that it's perfectly acceptable to use a boxed pancake mix instead of making the batter from scratch. You will however have to prepare the Lingonberries which is very simple. Follow instructions on box, make pancakes, top with Lingonberries.

At The BIG LEBOWSKI'S POOL

Bunny: Blow on them.

Dude: You want me to blow on your Toes?

Bunny: I can't Blow that Far! (Yeah we Bet! Ha ha!)

Dude: Oh, you're Bunny!

Bunny: I'll S_ck your C_ _k for $1,000 …

(Brandt Chuckles)

Brandt: Marvelous woman. We all love her.

Bunny: But Brandt can't watch or he has to pay
a hundred.

Dude: You sure he won't mind? (Dude says
referring to guy in the pool)

Bunny: Uli doesn't care about anything.
He's a Nihilist.

Dude: Must be Exhausting!

FRENCH TOAST

French Toast, or should I say "Freedom Toast?" Dudes says this was "Fancy Food" when he was a kid. A special treat that he has always loved. Doesn't eat it all the time, maybe once a month. Keeps it more special that way. Dude may have it on its own or with a couple little Breakfast Sausages on the side. It's a classic that Dude has loved all his life. How bout you? You can even top the French Toast with Longonberries if you have any left over after making Lingonberry Pancakes.

Abide in your Breakfast, the most important meal of the day.

FRENCH TOAST DUDES WAY

Recipe for 2 People;

3-4 Large Eggs
6 slices White Bread
Butter, Cinnamon
Syrup of Your Choice .. Real Maple Syrup is Best,
but the Dude might at times settle for a
.99 cent Discount Syrup. That's OK !
¼ cup Milk

1. Beat Milk, Eggs, and ½ teaspoon of Cinnamon in a medium sized bowl.

2. Heat a large frying pan on low flame.

3. Dip bread into beaten egg mixture 2 at a time. Add 2 tablespoons butter to pan.

4. Put two slices of bread or as much as will fit into the size pan you have at a time into the pan. Let cook about two minutes on each side over a low flame. Remove slices of French Toast to plates as they are finished.

5. Spread pats of butter over each slice of French Toast if you like. Pour Syrup over French Toast and Relish the moment!

NOTE: Some sliced Strawberries, Banana, or Mixed Berries served alongside the French Toast makes a great accompaniment. And Sausages or Bacon is Cool too!

TUNA ???
"Canned Man"

Tuna? Along with Donny, Walter, Smokey, maybe Brandt, and a host of others, Tuna is one of "The Dudes Best Friends" and has been kind and served Dude well over the years. What's better than Tuna, The Dude has often said. It'll feed you right cheap, "Fuckin Eh." It's always there, it's easy, doesn't give you a hard time, and it taste good too.

The can is small, classic and lovely, a can of Tuna is. No matter if it's Chicken of the Sea, Bumble Bee or good ole Star-Kist "Charlie Tuna." Six-and-a-half ounces of pure joy and nourishment in those lovely little cans, that's affordable and convenient as heck. Dude loves them so. Yes the can is little, and Dude doesn't normally like to do this, but in tough times, when money was super low and the Unemployment Checks ran out, Dude was able to go into a supermarket and easily put a can in his pocket, paying at the counter for the quart of Milk for the Caucasians, but for some reason, completely forgetting about the can of Tuna in his pocket. And nobody said anything, so, oh well, Fuck-It Man!

Yes, the Dude sure loves his Tuna and a nice classic Tuna Sandwich or his renowned Macaroni and Tuna Salad. It's Yummy!

Tuna is big in America. Canned Tuna in itself is pretty iconic. A lot of people like to make Tuna Casserole, but canned Tuna is pretty much used for one thing about 98% of the time, and that's to make a good ole American Tuna-Fish Sandwich. And this is how

Dude likes to eat his Tuna a good amount of the time he pulls one of those little suckers out. But Dude likes it one other way a whole-lot and his use of canned tuna is pretty much split down the middle. Half the time The Dude makes Tuna Salad and Tuna Sandwiches with the Tuna Salad. The other half of the time, The Dude has a great old family recipe that he's been eating since he's a kid. It's his family's recipe for *Macaroni and Tuna Salad*, and The Dude eats quite a good bit of it to this very day. It is super simple, "Low-Brow" and inexpensive, yet quite tasty and satisfying. This Macaroni and Tuna Salad is quick and easy to prepare, like most of The Dudes favorite collected recipes are. And of course it has to be tasty and economical. And The Dude so generously wants to share it with you. Dude thinks you're gonna be quite surprised at this one, the simplicity and tastiness. You make yourself a two or three can batch and you're gonna be able to have lunch and numerous meals or snacks out of it. It's especially great to have on hand in the *frig* where you can grab it any time you get a little twang of hunger. Dude says, it's an absolute must you make this one. He's sure you're gonna love it and make it for years to come. And you'll think about your ole pal Duder every time you have it. Abide!

Classic Tuna Salad "Dudes Way"

Ingredients:

2 cans of TUNA (whichever one is on sale)
½ cup Real Mayonnaise (buy the brand on sale)
1 tablespoon of Dijon or Guldens Mustard (optional)
½ teaspoon ground Black Pepper
1 celery stalk cut into a small dice (optional)

1. Open cans of Tuna and drain off the water or oil. Place drained tuna in a large mixing bowl.

2. Add mayonnaise, mustard (optional), Black Pepper, and Celery (optional) and mix with a wooden spoon until all ingredients are incorporated together.

3. Your Tuna Salad is now ready to be used to make a quick and easy Tuna Sandwich. You can toast the bread or not. The Tuna Sandwich is great with a couple pieces of Boston or other Lettuce and or Tomato. I like to cut about six slices of cucumber to put on the sandwich.

NOTE: You only need three ingredients to make the most Basic Tuna Salad; the Tuna, Black Pepper, and Mayonnaise, anything else is optional. Other Items you can add to the Basic Tuna Salad Recipe are, a bit of Mustard, One Hard Boiled Egg to every 2 cans of Tuna, Peas, or diced boiled potato. Experiment with whatever you like. These extra items are usually cheaper than Tuna and will make the tuna salad even more economical than it already is.

"The Dudes life-long Love of Throwing a Hard and Heavy-Ball down a hard-wood floor (Alley) at a Bunch of Pins, trying to knock down as many as possible, and the Dream of the elusive Perfect 300 Game. Bowling!"

DBZ   2012 NYC

DUDE'S MACARONI & TUNA SALAD

If you only learn how to make this dish and just a few others, you will be doing quite alright and will be able to save a good amount of money and time as well.

Dude learned how to make this dish when he was just 12 years old. He still makes it quite often till this very day. It's something he likes to have on hand as often as possible. When it's there, any time ole Duder gets the munchies, all Dude has to do is reach in the frig and grab a bowl of the tasty stuff, enjoy and Abide he does. Dude's Mom used to make it and he has always loved this combination of tuna, macaroni and mayo, with some crunchy fresh Celery to boot. It is quick and easy to make and takes just about 15 minutes to put together. Make a big bowl to keep on had, and whenever you get a little hungry, it's right there in the frig, ready to go.

DUDES MACARONI & TUNA SALAD

INGREDIENTS:

2 cans TUNA (use whatever brand is on sale)
1 lb. Elbow Macaroni
3 Celery Stalks cut into medium dice
¾ cup good quality Mayonnaise
2 tablespoons Gulden's or Dijon Mustard
½ teaspoon Salt and 1 teaspoon ground Black Pepper

PREPARATION for MAC & TUNA

1. Boil Elbow Macaroni according to directions on package.

2. While macaroni is cooking, open tuna cans. Drain them of all water or oil in can. Place Tuna, celery, Mustard, Mayonnaise, salt, & pepper in a large mixing bowl and mix all ingredients together.

3. When macaroni has finished cooking, remove from stove and drain. Run cold water over macaroni for about 3 minutes. Drain all water off of macaroni in a colander or wire strainer.

4. Add cooked cooled Macaroni in bowl with Tuna and other ingredients and mix thoroughly with a large spoon. You're finished. Place the Macaroni &Tuna Salad in a large sealed container and let cool in the refrigerator, and you're set.

So there you have it friend, The Dudes Famous Macaroni and Tuna Salad. It's Awesome! Dude's glad you tried it and just knows you're gonna love this baby a long-long-time, just like Ole Duder. Enjoy!

PS .. A little Dude advice. Dude suggest whenever you see a good deal (Sale) on canned Tuna at Ralph's or your favorite supermarket, pick-up a few cans, stock up and save. Five cans of sale priced tuna at .79 cents a can is just $3.95 . Those same 5 cans at regular price of $1.29, or $6.45 total. Pretty smart, keep doing that, and... Abide in that!

"If you *Will It* Dude, it is No Dream"

Walter Sobchak

DUDE COOKING SCHOOL
"Duder Method"

"Ha-Ha, not really, just a little Humor from
The Cowboy Stranger" In actuality it does
have some truth to it. Keep Her Goin."

Yes you can call this Dude Cooking School if you like. It almost is. The Dudes recipes and great advice, he's definitely teaching you a thing or two, if you're a novice cook or absolute beginner. Even if you're not, and you happen to be a top Professional Chef, you probably can learn a thing or two from "The Dude," a-few-ins-a-few-outs, a few what-have-yous, "The Usual." So far, you've learned how to cook eggs and home fries. You've now got down Tuna Salad and the classic Tuna Sandwich along with the great and wonderful "Dude Mac and Tuna Salad." It's a real winner and with these, and once you know how to make Tomato Sauce and Soups which are very easy, economical, and very good and healthy. Time savers too as you make one large batch and get about 12 meals or so out of them.

Next is Chili, one of Dudes favorites and a Bedrock of his cooking philosophy and repertoire, for once you got Chili down, you can have a bowl of Chili, Chili con Carne, Burritos, Tacos, and the famed Dude Chili and Cheese Omelet. Right on! Move on and forward, you're moving on up.

CHILI

Chili, "It's as American as Apple Pie." More so! Chili? It's an All American favorite. It's versatile, economical, and "Oh so Tasty!" It's easy to make, stores well, and once it is made, you can make an array of other dishes like; Chili Dogs, Tacos and Burritos based on the Chili. And that my friends is why The Dude loves his Chili so. Dude goes to Ralph's, picks up all the necessary ingredients, Ground Chuck, tomatoes, onions, and what not. He's already got the Cumin, salt, and peppers on hand. He got all his stuff, throws some Creedence on the stereo, chops up some onions and garlic, browns the beef, gets everything in the pot, and it's off to simmer.

Once everything is in the pot, the Dude sets the heat to a very low flame and lets the Chili simmer for about an hour and fifteen. While the Chili simmers away, Dude is free to kick back and relax, listening to Creedence, sometimes he'll do a bit of Tai Chi for ten minutes or so, make a Caucasian, then sit back and relax as the Chili simmers away. It's all very Zen. Dude digs this ritual and is happy in his thoughts of that wonderful pot of Chili and its net results. Once done, Dude has some small flour tortillas all ready with some grated Cheddar Cheese, chopped fresh onions and fresh tomato, maybe a bit of fresh Cilantro. When the Chili finished, Dude turns the flame off and goes to town right away. He grabs a beer and assembles a platter of 3 tasty Tacos.

Dude will take a third to have the Chili, put in sealable containers and freeze it. This he'll pull out of the freezer in about 10 days or so. Thaws it, and he's already to make some Tacos or Burritos. He's already done most of the work a week and a have before. The other half of the Chili he puts in containers and into the frig so he has his Chili on hand to make Tacos, Burritos, and Chili Cheese Omelets for the next 3 or 4 days. Dude will then take a break from the Chili items for maybe 3 or 4 days, and when he wants he's already got the Chili on hand in the freezer that he made a week or so before. Just has to thaw it out and after that, it's a couple tasty tacos in a few minutes flat. Pretty Smart? Dude got methods, and if you follow the Dudes lead, you'll eat a lot of tasty stuff, save money, and save time. More time for; "Fuck it Dude, let's go Bowling," as Walter would say.

"That's just like your Opinion Man!"

The Dude

DUDES COWBOY CHILI

Dude got this recipe from a friend of his at the Bowling Alley. A guy who never bowled himself but hung out at the bar, drinking Sioux City Sarsaparilla. He had a big thick Salt & Pepper Mustache and wore a big ass cowboy hat and Cowboy Garb. The cowboy at the bar (The Cowboy Stranger) was pretty cool. He got the Dudes stamp of approval, so you know he's cool. Dude and the Stranger would sit around, Dude drinking a White Russian ("I'll have another Caucasian Gary") and the Stranger sipping on his Sarsaparilla. These two had conversations on all sorts of things. One day the conversation turned to Chili and Tacos. The Cowboy said he didn't eat tacos all that much, but he did make a killer Chili. Dude and The Stranger talked Chili for a bit and the Dude liked what he heard. The Dude asked the Cowboy if he wouldn't mind giving him his Chili recipe.   The Cowboy obliged the Dude, and right then and there, wrote his excellent Chili recipe down for the Dude on a couple of cocktail napkins at the bar. The Dude pasted those napkins with the cowboys Killer Chili right into his spiral bound notebook, and the Dude has been making his Chili with this recipe ever since. The Dude passes it on to you to. Go forth young man, make Chili and multiply.

Dude knows Cowboys make the best Chili. That's why he was so anxious to get the recipe.

DUDES COWBOY CHILI

INGREDIENTS:

3 pounds ground Beef (Chuck is preferred)
4 medium Onions, cut into a medium dice
8 cloves of Garlic, peeled and minced
1-28 ounce can crushed Tomato
1 cup water
1 teaspoon Salt
2 tablespoons Cumin, 1 tablespoon Oregano
2 tablespoons Sweet Paprika
1 teaspoon Cayenne Pepper
1-2 teaspoons Hot Sauce (Tabasco, Louisiana Hot
Sauce, Crystal or which ever brand you like)
1 tablespoon Lea & Perrin's Worcestershire Sauce

CHILI COOKING PROCEDURE:

1. Get a large 6-8 quart pot and line the bottom with vegetable oil. Turn the flame to medium heat.

2. Add ground chop meat and cook for about 12 minutes until the meat loses its raw color. Turn off heat.

3. Put the meat in a colander to drain excess fat.

4. In the same large pot, add the onions and cook over medium heat for 5 minutes. Add the garlic cook for 3 minutes.
5. Add the ground meat back to the pot. Sprinkle the salt and   Black Pepper onto   the Beef and sauté for 2 minutes.

6. Add the tomatoes, oregano, Paprika, and Cumin. Turn the flame up to high until the ingredients start to bubble, lower the flame so the Chili will cook at a gentle simmer. Let simmer for 1 hour.

7. Add the Hot Sauce and Worcestershire Sauce and continue simmering the Chili for another ½ hour. The CHILI is now finished and ready to eat on its own or with a couple crushed Saltine Crackers, with rice and beans as Chili con Carne, or to make into Burritos or Tacos, or even a most outstanding Chili Dog. "Enjoy!"

If you want the Chili hotter, you can increase the amount of Cayenne and Tabasco or other Hot Sauce. In Dudes recipe here, he makes it so you can just start to discern that it is just slightly hot, but not really too hot. This is the way Dude likes it. Later on when he's making a Taco or Chili Dog with his Chili and he's in the mood to have it a bit hotter he can always add a bit of Hot Sauce then and there. If the Chili is made very hot, you can never take the hot out, but you can always add some later. You catch The Dudes drift?

NOTE on The CHILI: This is a large recipe. Dude makes a recipe large, as he wants to help you save time as well as a lot of MONEY. You take two hours one time to make the batch of Chili that you will cook that evening, and you will have quite a lot left to put into containers in both the refrigerator and freezer. You're gonna get about 20 meals out of this recipe. See that, take two hours one time, and for 20 meals, you won't need to hardly cook   at all,   just a few minutes preparation afterwards.

You will then have Chili that is ready to make into Tacos, Burritos, 3 Way Chili, Chili Dogs, or just a Bowl of Chili with Cheese and fresh onions in a matter of minutes at any time. "Voila.

3 WAY CHILI

Three Way Chili? It's a great way to serve Chili The Dudes says. And The Stranger says, "It stretches Her Out," the Chili that is. "3 Way Chili" is a beloved staple of the great Mid-Western City of Cincinnati. Dude found the recipe that was a clipped out of an article, sandwiched between a book on Bowling that the Dude bought at a "Garage Sale" when he was driving around listening to Creedence tapes while toking on a Dubey one day. The book and the free recipe inside, was just 25 cents. Dude thought the recipe to be quite interesting and a good way to stretch Chili with some inexpensive costing Spaghetti which he buys on sale at Ralph's for just .69 cents a box.

So, you ask ole Duder, "How do you make this Cincinnati 3 Way Chili." Quite simple. Get yourself some shredded Cheddar Cheese, cook up some spaghetti, drain it, put it on a plate, and top with some Cowboy Chili and then some Cheddar Cheese. Sit back and Enjoy!

3 WAY CHILI

INGREDIENTS:

1 pound Spaghetti
4 Cups Dudes Cowboy Chili
8 ounces Yellow Cheddar Cheese, shredded
2 tablespoons Butter

Preparation:

1. Add Dudes Cowboy Chili to a small pot and heat over low heat for 10 minutes.

2. Bring 4 quarts salted water to the boil in a medium pot.

3. Add Spaghetti. Cook the spaghetti according to directions on package.

4. Drain the Spaghetti in a colander, reserving about 8 tablespoons of cooking water.

5. Put the spaghetti back in the pot it cooked in with the reserved cooking water. Add butter and mix. Add half of the Chili to Spaghetti and mix.

6. Serve 4 equal portions of Spaghetti and Chili on 4 plates. Divide remaining Chili evenly on top of the 4 plates. Top the spaghetti & chili evenly with the grated Cheddar Cheese. Serve and Enjoy!

BURRITOS & TACOS "DUDES WAY"

Burritos & Tacos. What the difference, some would ask? What's the difference? Most know, as does The Dude, but in case you're from Bum F_ck, Iowa, or you just don't know, here goes. Well, they are both made from Tortillas that are made of either Corn or Flour. Dude usually prefers Flour Tortillas. Tacos are a smaller Tortilla that are filled with various Meat, Vegetable, Fish, and or Poultry, or just about anything you want to throw in them. You fill the tortillas with your fillings of choice, fold in half and eat.

Burritos are larger Tortillas, made mostly of Flour, but can be corn. Burritos can have the same multitude of ingredients, whatever the person making or eating the Burrito decides on.

Where the Taco is filled with the ingredients and folded in half, a Burrito is packages to completely envelope the contents inside. The Burrito also may have rice inside, which Tacos usually do not have.

Also, one Burrito should be enough for a full serving, were as with Tacos you usually need Two or Three to make a meal and they may be of one, two, or three different types. Maybe; one Pork, one with Beef, and one Grilled Chicken Taco. On the Baja Peninsular in Mexico and in San Diego, California where the Dude, Donny, and Walter have been known to make many a road trip to, the Fish Taco "Rains Supreme" and is most popular in these areas. Yes the Dudes clunker was able to make it there and back, a number of times.

Yes, our hero "The Dude" really loves his Tacos and Burritos, most Los Angelinos (all Californians) do. Dude loves all kinds of Tacos and Burritos, filled with Chicken , Pork, Fish or what-not, and Dude eats all of them. But when it comes to eating Tacos and Burritos at home, most often with the Dude, they are Chili Cheese Tacos or Chili, Rice, Bean, and Cheese Burritos. The reason is simple. Dude loves making his Cowboy Chili, and once Dude has a batch made, it's Chili and Cheese Burritos all the way. They're easy, once Dude has his Chili that is.

DUDES CHILI CHEESE QUESADILLA

Quesadillas are a great item to serve at a party, along with Guacamole, and perhaps some Chili con Carne or one of The Dudes favorite Chicken-Wings Recipes, as the main event. Dude often likes to make a Quesadilla and have it along with two Fried Eggs for breakfast or anytime of the day. "A great combo!" says ole Duder.

To make a Quesadilla, simply take one or more large flour tortillas, sprinkle grated Cheddar, Monterey Jack or some type Mexican Cheese over the top. Put some heated Chili on top of Cheese in spots here and there, not over the whole tortilla completely. Put on a sheet pan and heat in a 375 degree oven for about 6 minutes. Remove from oven, fold the Quesadilla in half so it is in the shape of a half circle. Place on cutting board and cut the Quesadilla into about 6 pie-shaped wedges. Serve immediately. Enjoy!

GUACAMOLE "The Dudes Way"

Hey Man, it's California, it's LA, Dudes a slacker Hippy. Of course he likes his "Guac." Dude got this recipe from his buddy Juan. And it's a good one. Serve in a bowl at a party with Tortilla Chips, or add to the filling of any type of Taco or Burrito you like.

INGREDIENTS:

1/2 cup finely chopped white onion

2 Jalapeño Peppers, seeded and minced

2 tbsp. finely chopped Fresh Cilantro

Salt, a pinch

2 medium Hass Avocados (ripe)

2 Plum Tomato, chopped to a medium dice

1. Cut Avocados in half. Remove the pit. Scoop out pulp and put into a medium size glass mixing bowl.

2. Mash avocado with a potato-masher or back of a wooden spoon to break down the avocado.

3. Add all remaining ingredients and mix with a wooden spoon.

4. Serve with Tortilla Chips, and or use as an ingredient for Burritos & Tacos. And Enjoy!

SOUP

SOUP! It's a Good Thing" The Dude just loves Soup, its Ease of Preparation, it's affordability, Health aspects (Soup is Good for The Dude and YOU Too), and it's Time Saving properties. Yes the Dude loves his soup. He grew up with it. Lots of Campbell's Soup served day and night by mother Lebowski; Chicken Noodle, Tomato with crackers of course, Beef Barley, and Dudes childhood favorite (at the time) Cream of Mushroom. Dudes Mom occasionally made homemade soup like Beef Barley or Split Pea, but it was mostly Campbell's or Progresso Soup in the Lebowski household. Yes the Dude's family ate mostly Campbell Soup with the occasional homemade one. And the Dude loves and cherishes those days of childhood, Campbell's Soup, playing Wiffle Ball, going to the movies, and the beginnings of The Dudes life-long love of throwing a hard and heavy ball down a hard-wood floor (alley) at a bunch of pins, trying to knock down as many as possible, and the Dream of the elusive Perfect 300 Game. Bowling.

Yes the Dude loved his can of Campbell Soup, the can looks so Cool. Andy even made it an Iconic Peace of American Pop Art. Yes, these iconic cans are a piece of art in themselves, and just looking at a can gives the Dude goose-bumps, iconic American that the Dude loves and cherishes so, same as a bottle of Heinz Ketchup. Ever really stop and look at a bottle of Heinz Ketchup? It's a thing of beauty. Seriously! The design, form, the colors chosen, fonts, the way the glass cut bottle. You think I'm crazy? Ask the Dude. He feels the same way about that lovely little bottle of American made Ketchup. Spam too. A thing of beauty and venerable versatility

The Dude loves his soup. But he has graduated from those mostly Campbell's Soup days. Though Dude loves the beloved Campbell's Soup and memories of eating it in his childhood, he eventually came to know that there is a much better alternative and one The Dude really loves, and that's nice pot and bowl of homemade. Homemade Soup. Very good and healthy for you, they taste good, they are inexpensive and very easy to make. And Dude likes all these attributes of soup. The Dude always has a can or two of Campbell's Cream of Mushroom (Dudes all-time favorite), Chicken Noodle, or Tomato (to go with his Grilled Cheese). Dude prefers homemade soup, but every now and then to reminisce, he'll have a can of Campbell's.

So the Dude ate a lot of Campbell's Soup as a child, but once he got out of college, was living life and especially during his "Roadie Days" on the Speed of Sound Tour with those "Bunch of Asshole" in Metalica, the Dude discovered a lot of good soups, Homemade ones and there many virtues. Dude loved going to different diners and road houses, having a cup of Coffee and whatever the Homemade Soup of the day was. The soups where tasty and satisfy, and the best priced (cheapest) thing on the menu. That's all the Dude needed. An endless Cup of Joe, a tasty steamy bowl of the Homemade Soup of The Day, complete with bread & butter, and Saltine Crackers too. What a deal. Our hero "The Dude" started collecting great homemade soup recipes.

Dudes favorite soups are; Split Pea, Chicken Noodle, and one his buddy Danny gave him (that's me)

Got Any Kahlua?

Bozos Manhattan Clam Chowder, which Dude makes on special occasions and especially loves it in the hot months of Summer, always with visions of the Sea Shore and his relaxation cassette tapes of Seagulls squawking against the back drop of ocean waves crashing against the beach. And the Dude doesn't mind taking a few tokes of Thai Stick to precipitate the relaxation along the way. Dude says Bozos Clam Chowder is right yummy, Donny agrees too.

So, as the Dude says, learn a few soups. They're the easiest things in the world to make. You through a few things in the pot, let it simmer a bit, and you'll be set with 12 servings or so of tasty, economical, time saving, healthy soup. It's a Bed-Rock of the Dudes culinary repertoire and Dude wants you to make it yours too. Abide!

Dude: *Yeah Man! It really tied the room together!*

Donny: *What tied the room together Dude?*

Dude: *My Rug!*

Walter: *Were you listening to The Dudes story Donny?*

Donny : *I was Bowling.*

Walter: *So you have no frame of reference here. You're like a little child who wonders in to a movie!*

DUDES SPLIT PEA SOUP

INGREDIENTS:

1 medium Onion, peeled and finely Diced
1 ½ tablespoons Vegetable Oil (Canola,
Corn Oil, etc.)
1 Carrot peeled and cut to medium dice
1 Russet or Idaho Potato, peeled and
and cut to medium dice (Optional)
1 pound bag of dry Split Peas
¼ pound Ham, diced
Salt and Black Pepper to taste

1. Place oil and onions in a 6 quart pot. Cook over medium heat for 2 minutes. Add ham and sauté for 2 minutes.

2. Add all remaining ingredients to pot.

3. Add enough water to cover 1 inch past all ingredients. Bring up to the boil over high heat. When ingredients come to the boil, lower heat to low. Cook for about 1 ½ hours, stirring occasionally and making sure to keep soup at a low simmer.

5. The soup is done when all the Split Peas have liquefied.

6. Serve with Croutons or Bread. Save remaining soup in sealed containers to eat at later dates.

MANHATTAN CLAM
CHOWDER
"BOZO'S"

This is a great soup that was quite popular when The Dude was a kid, Manhattan Clam Chowder that is. For some reason, unfortunately its popularity has waned. Maybe as a result of New England Clam Chowder being the far more popular of the two, even in Manhattan by God.

Dude thinks it is high time the popularity of Manhattan Clam Chowder is revived to the status that it so deservedly had Once Upon a Time. The Dude wants you to help in the quest, his wish. So Dude asks you all to Abide, make this tasty soup, Bozos Clam Chowder, enjoy it and share it with friends and family. Have a party that revolves around the Clam Chowder. Serve Pigs-In-A-Blanket and or Guacamole as starters, Bozos Clam Chowder as the main event, and finished up with some store bought pound cake "Gussied Up" with Dudes Kahlua Hot Fudge Sauce and you'll have a party your friends will not forget soon. And please don't forget the White Russians.

Dude says this recipe is very easy, though to a beginner cook it may seem a little daunting, especially the cooking of the clams. It's not. If you master this recipe, you might gain a little fame, and it is worth it. And The Dude will appreciate that you've joined him in spreading the word of Bozos Clam Chowder. The Dude will recognize you for this heroic deed, and he'll welcome you into his World. And what a lovely World it is, "Dudes-World-Dudes-World-Dudes-World." Ha-ha!

Dude says that Bozos Manhattan Clam Chowder is great to make for a Potluck Dinner, and for all events, even in large quantities, especially for a backyard barbecue, or Bowling League Championship Party.

So The Dude says abide in making the Clam Chowder and spreading its word, Manhattan Clam Chowder that is, and "No Cream Allowed."

Note: Where'd it get its name? Bozos Manhattan Clam Chowder, you might be asking? Bozo was the Fire Chief of the local Fire Department where little Jeffrey Lebowski grew up. We won't reveal the Fire Chief's real name, but he nickname was, of course, Bozo. Don't ask, we don't know why. We just know his nickname, Bozo and that he made a mean Clam Chowder that he made for the many Fire House picnics, gatherings, and all sorts of family and fire house events. Bozo's Clam Chowder was the best around, and he was quite famous for it, thus the recipe. That's about all we know. Dude got the recipe, he loves it, and makes it all the time, and he's passing it on to you, dear achiever, follower of The Dude. Abide!

The CLAM CHOWDER … "Bozo's"

INGREDIENTS:

You can double or triple the recipe to make
even more.

12 Quahog Clams (Chowder Clams) washed
4 slices of Bacon cut into ¼" dice
1 medium Onion diced
2 stalks of Celery, diced
2 Carrots, peeled and cut to medium dice
1 Green Bell Pepper, seeded and diced
1 small Bottle of Clam Juice
3 large Idaho Potatoes, peeled and diced
1 28 can whole Tomatoes roughly chopped
6 cups of water
¼ teaspoon Thyme, Salt & Black Pepper
1 Bay Leave

1. Place clams in a large 8 Qt. size pot. Add 1 ½ cups
water.

2. Cover the pot with a lid. Turn heat on to a high flame
and cook until all the clam shells have opened. About 6
minutes.

3. Turn off heat. Place clams with the cooking liquid in
a large bowl. Let cool.

4. Rinse the pot with water and place back on the stove.
5. Turn heat on to medium and add the Bacon and cook
for about 4 to 5 minutes, stirring with a wooden spoon.

The Bacon will render its fat. Remove half the fat from the pot and discard.

6. Add Onion and Green Pepper. Sauté for 4 minutes.
7. Add Celery, Carrots, water, tomatoes, and potatoes. Turn heat up to high and bring to the boil. As soon as contents comes the boil, lower the heat so contents is at a medium simmer.

8. Add bay Leaf, Thyme, Salt & Pepper to taste. Simmer for 25 minutes.

9. While the soup is simmering, remove the Clams from their shell. Chop the clams into ¼" dice.

10. After the soup has simmered, add the chopped Clams and clam cooking liquid. Simmer for 4 minutes over very low heat. Serve as is or with Oyster Crackers.

"He thinks Carpet Pissers did this?"

Dude to Brandt

DUDES CHICKEN POSOLE

Dude got this recipe from his Mexican friend Rubin. It's easy to make, super tasty, nourishing, and like all soups, it re-heats well. It's Mexican and Dude loves that.

Ingredients:

2 Tablespoons Olive Oil
1 large Onion, peeled and diced
4 cloves fresh Garlic, peeled and minced fine
1 28 oz. can whole Tomatoes
1 tablespoon Oregano
1 tablespoon Black Pepper
1 tablespoon Smoked Paprika
1 Tbs. ground Cumin
1 ½ teaspoons Salt
32 ounces low sodium Chicken Broth
3 cups water
5 boneless Chicken Breast
2 – 15 oz. cans Hominy (Posole), drained
1 can Kernel Corn, drained

Garnishes:

2 Limes, sliced for garnish
Tortilla Chips for garnish
8 Radishes, sliced for garnish

PREPARATION:

1. Place olive oil and onions in a large pot. Cook on low heat for 4 minutes. Add Garlic and cook 3 minutes.

2. Add Oregano, Salt, Black Pepper, Cumin, and Paprika. Cook on low heat 1 minute.

3. Add tomatoes, turn heat to high and cook 2-3 minutes.

4. Add chicken broth and cook on high heat until all comes to the boil. Add chicken breast.

5. When all comes back to a boil, lower heat so broth is simmering. Let simmer for 10 minutes, until chicken breast are fully cooked inside.

6. Remove all the chicken breast from pot and set aside to cool.

7. Add Posole and canned Corn to pot. Let cook at medium simmer for 10 minutes.

8. Shred chicken breast and add to pot. Cook as very low simmer for 7 minutes.

The Posole is ready. Serve each guest a nic bowl with a good amount of chicken and posole in each bowl. Place limes, radishes, and tortilla chips on side for each person to garnish themselves.

Walter's Jewish Penicillin
a.k.a. CHICKEN NOODLE SOUP

Chicken Noodle Soup, they call it "Jewish Penicillin." Dude believes it. He has eaten it when he had some terrible colds, and it always made The Dude feel a whole lot better. It's tasty and most nutritious, and it warms the Cockles of Your Heart, The Dude says.

Can you guess where The Dude got this recipe for Jewish Penicillin? That's' right, from Walter who in practicing Shomer Shabbos Walter says he doesn't *Fucking Roll* on Saturday! "Shomer Shabbos."

Donny: "How come you don't Bowl on Saturdays Walter?"

Walter: "Saturday Donny is Shabbos, the Jewish Day of rest. I don't drive a Car, I don't ride in a car, I don't handle Money, I don't turn on the oven, and I Sure as Shit DON'T FUCKIN ROLL" !!!!!

Donny: "Jeeze" !!!

Walter: "Shomer Shabbos"

Dude: "Walter how am I gonna …."

Walter: "Shomer FUCKING SHABBOS" !!!!

Recipe : WALTER'S JEWISH PENICILLIN
"CHICKEN NOODLE SOUP"

This is actually two recipes in one, "Almost." In this recipe for Chicken Noodle Soup you will cook a whole chicken. You will use the cooked chicken breast for Chicken Salad and the rest of the chicken, the legs and thighs will go into the soup. That's awesome Dude!!!

Ingredients:

1 whole roasting Chicken 4-5 pounds
2 medium Onions cut into a medium dice
5 whole cloves of garlic, Peeled
6 stalks of Celery cut into large cube
6 Carrots cut into a large dice
6 quarts of water
1 pound package of Egg Noodles
1 Bay Leaf, 1 teaspoon Salt
½ teaspoon Black Pepper

Cooking Procedures:

1. Fill a large 8 qt. Pot with water. Wash the chicken and place it into the pot. Cover the pot. Turn on the flame and bring the water to the boil. Once the water reaches the boiling point, lower the flame so the water simmers at a slow simmer.

2. Add the carrots, celery, garlic, onions, Bay Leaf, salt, and pepper to the pot.

3. Let the soup simmer for 1 hour and 15 minutes.

4. Remove the chicken from the pot and let it cool down.

5. While the chicken is cooling, cook the Egg Noodles according to the directions on the package. Drain the

noodles, then sprinkle with a little olive oil so the noodles won't stick together.

6. Once the chicken has cooled down, remove the breast and reserve to make chicken salad with.

7. Pick all the rest of the meat off the chicken bones and put into the soup pot. Let the chicken meat simmer in the pot for ten minutes.

8. Add the noodles and let simmer for 2 minutes. The soup is now ready to serve.

NOTE: If you'd like you can substitute rice for the noodles to make Chicken and Rice Soup. To do so, cook one cup of rice in 2 ½ cups water for 15 minutes and drain. At the point where you take the chicken out of the pot, you will put the rice into the pot of soup and let simmer 5 minutes.

DUDE MEETS KNOX

Knox: What do you do Lebowski?

Dude: Who The FUCK are You? !!!

Knox: A friend of Maudy's ..

Dude: A friend with a Cleft ASSHOLE ???

(Knox Giggles)

CHICKEN SALAD

Chicken Salad Sandwiches are a nice thing to eat every now and then, especially in the summer when you don't feel like cooking much and don't want a hot stove on.

When you have Chicken Salad, you can make one of Bunny Lebowski's Chicken Salad Sandwiches. Bunny has her sandwiches on Whole Wheat Bread, Dude has his on White, and you know what Walter has his on don't you? That's right, Jewish Rye.

1. To make the Chicken Salad, simply dice the cooked chicken breast that you have from making your chicken soup. Place in a mixing bowl. Add ¾ of real Mayonnaise, ¼ teaspoon ground Black Pepper, and ½ a cup of diced celery.

2. Mix all the ingredients together with a wooden spoon.

3. The Chicken Salad is and ready to be spread on to 2 pieces of White Bread, Whole Wheat, or Rye. "Shomer Shabbos!"

If you'd like, you can dress the sandwich with a couple pieces of Boston or other lettuce and a slice or two of fresh ripe tomato. You should be able to make Four or Five Sandwiches.

NOTE: If you are not making Chicken Soup and just want to make Chicken Salad from scratch, poach two chicken breasts in slowly simmering water for 10-12 minutes. Let cool to room temperature. Mix with mayonnaise, celery, and pepper. You can make double the portion to be able to make 8-10 sandwiches by cooking four chicken breasts and adding more celery and more mayonnaise. "Enjoy!"

EGG SALAD *&* BUNNY'S COUNTRY CLUB SANDWICHES

Egg Salad is a great item. Dude sure thinks so. When you have Egg Salad on hand, you can make nice quick and easy Sandwiches. You could also compose a nice Summer Platter of Egg Salad with cold steamed Green Beans and Carrots with slices of juicy Ripe Tomato and Cucumber over Boston Lettuce.

The Dudes recipe below will make 5-6 Egg Salad Sandwiches. The sandwiches are best made with good quality white bread or whole wheat and you can make them with or without sliced tomato and or lettuce.

And an Egg Salad Sandwich is just the type of thing that "That Slut" Bunny Lebowski likes to eat poolside while The Nihilist is lounging in the pool, Brandt is running around doing things for The Big Lebowski, and the Dude states his case and picks up a Rug.

"It really tied the room together."

EGG SALAD INGREDIENTS:

6 Extra Large Eggs
1 cup Mayonnaise
2 tablespoons Dijon Mustard (optional)
½ teaspoon ground Black Pepper and a pinch of Salt

PREPARATION:

1. Place Eggs in a pot with enough water to cover pass the eggs by a half-inch or so. Bring the water to the boil. Lower water to a gentle simmer and let the eggs cook for 8 minutes.

2. Turn flame off and drain the hot water from the pan. Leave the eggs in the pot and run cold water over the eggs for two minutes. Drain off water and let eggs cool in the refrigerator for about 45 minutes.

3. Peel shells off the cooled boiled eggs. Slice eggs in half and put the yolks in a mixing bowl and the white on a cutting board.

4. Mash the yolks with a fork. Add the mustard, salt, pepper, and half the mayonnaise to the bowl and mix.

5. Chop the egg whites on a cutting board into a 1/8 inch dice.

6. Add the chopped egg whites and the remainder of the mayonnaise to the mixing bowl with egg yolk mixture and mix together.

7. The Egg Salad is done and ready to be made into sandwiches or to be one component of a cold composed Salad Plate.

Make Country Club Sandwiches with White or Whole Wheat Bread. Use Chicken or Egg Salad, with some Boston Lettuce and a slice of ripe tomato.

SPAGHETTI with TOMATO SAUCE

Spaghetti? Tomato Sauce? Spaghetti! Spaghetti with Tomato Sauce, is a major cornerstone of the Dudes cooking World and subsistence ever since college days. Sure the Dudes Mom fed him a lot of it in childhood too. What warm blooded American Child doesn't like it? And little Jeffrey Lebowski (before he Became "The Dude") sure liked his. It's super economical and always helped to stretch the Lebowski food budget, spaghetti was an still is super cheap and so were the jars of tomato sauce, and Jeffrey and the rest of the kids just loved it. Dudes mom never made tomato sauce from scratch like her son the Dude does now. He used to eat over his Italian-Americans friend homes, and always liked the real Home-Made thing made by an Italian-Mamma much better than the jar stuff.

So when The Dude asked his buddy Tony for a recipe, Tony was happy to oblige and instruct the Dude on a proper, and all- important Sugo di Pomodoro. That's Tomato Sauce to The Dude and the rest of you.

Spaghetti with Tomato Sauce is a huge favorite of most American kids. They Love it. In fact it may very well be after Burgers and the Classic "Peanut Butter and Jelly Sandwich," the number 3 most popular thing for the American children to eat. What they Love best "SKETTYS" as many kids call it.

Yes, Spaghetti with Tomato Sauce is quick and effortless to prepare. Get a loaf of Italian Bread, make a nice tossed salad of crispy Iceberg Lettuce, Tomato, and Zesty Fresh Cucumbers with some Wishbone Italian

Dressing and the family meal was completely set. It cost back then in the 50s and 60s just about .50 cents per family member including beverage, and Kool-Aid for the kids.

Now, some things you should know. In Italy Spaghetti Pomodoro (Spaghetti with Tomato) is held in great reverence. Spaghetti Pomodoro is to Italians what the Hamburger is to Americans, their single most popular dish. But Spaghetti Pomodoro in comparison is actually much more versatile then our beloved Hamburger, as by adding one or two other ingredients, you can make 1,000 other different dishes that stem from this one base dish. The Burger though it is wonderful and one of America's most beloved and cherished of all food items, and you can add a multitude of toppings, the great American Burger is nowhere near being as economical as Italian Tomato Sauce and all it's many off-shoots.

Tomato Sauce and especially Tomato Sauce with Spaghetti or other pasta is quite easy to prepare. You can even Make home-made Spaghetti-O's, with or without Hot-Dogs. They're inexpensive and fairly easy and quick to prepare. And once you have your basic Tomato Sauce you can make a number of different sauces and dishes from it, simply by changing or adding different ingredients.

A couple examples of the previous mentioned statement. Once you have your basic Tomato Sauce you can quickly and easily have a Mushroom Sauce, Salsa al Funghi in Italian, or "Shroom Sauce" as The Dude calls it. You make the Mushroom Sauce (Shroom-Sauce) simply by adding some sautéed fresh mushrooms to your already made, basic tomato sauce. See how easy?

If you want to make Spaghetti Puttanesca the famed Neapolitan dish of Naples "Ladies of The Night" you simply sauté a bit of garlic in Olive Oil, add a pinch of Hot Red Pepper flakes, a couple chopped Anchovies, some pitted good quality Black or Green Olives, and Capers, sauté, then add a couple cups of basic tomato sauce and "Voila" you have Puttanesca Sauce all set to go. Add sautéed Zucchini, Sweet Red Peppers, Eggplant, and Sicilian Olives to the Tomato Sauce and you have sauce for Pasta al Sicilian. Get the drift? Once you have the base tomato sauce, you can make many different sauces and pasta dishes simply by adding different ingredients. Add some good fresh Italian Sweet or Hot Pork Sausage from your favorite Pork Store and you've got an Italian-American favorite in Maccheroni con Salsice, "Pasta with Sausage." Quite easy, and you can see why the Dude likes this sauce and wants you to learn it. Learn the simple tomato Sauce and simply by adding different ingredients you can easily make 25 different sauces. Twenty-Five different pasta dishes, "Pretty Nifty, eh?" And who doesn't like Italian Food, and often? And like all "Dude Dishes" and recipes, it's inexpensive, easy to prepare, "Tasty" quick, and flexible and it stores well.

So, what are you waiting for? Try your first batch of the *Dudes Italian Tomato Sauce*. Get a nice crusty loaf of Italian Bread, a bottle of Chianti, make a plate of Spaghetti Pomodoro and all will be fine in your world tonight.

SPAGHETTI w/ SAUCE
"TOMATO SAUCE"

Ingredients:

3-28 oz. cans of good quality Crushed Tomatoes
always buy them "when?" That's right, ON SALE
1 medium onion cut into a small dice
9 cloves of Garlic, peeled and finely diced
¼ cup Italian Olive Oil
¼ teaspoon of salt and ¼ teaspoon
of Crushed Red Pepper
14 fresh basil Leaves minced or
¼ teaspoon Dried Basil
1 lb. Of Dried Italian made Spaghetti
½ lb. Good quality grated Pecorino Romano
or Parmigiano Reggiano

1. Place Olive Oil and onions in at least a 3 Qt. Pot. Set on stove over a medium flame. Cook for 2 minutes, then add the minced garlic and cook for three minutes. Add the crushed red pepper and cook for 1 minute.

2. Add the tomatoes. Turn the flame up to high until the sauce comes to the boil. Lower heat to a very low flame. If you are using Dried Basil, you will add in now. If you are using fresh Basil you will add it in the last 10 minutes of cooking.

3. Simmer the sauce over low heat for about 30 minutes. Stir the sauce and the bottom of the pot with a wooden spoon every two minutes to keep the sauce from sticking to the bottom of the pot and burning.

4. The sauce is done after 30 minutes, turn the gas off.

5. To cook the Spaghetti you should have a large 6 qt. Pot filled with water. Bring the water to the boil and add 2 Tablespoon of salt to the water. Add the pasta and cook according to the directions on the package.

6. Drain the pasta in a colander then place the spaghetti in a large Pasta Serving Bowl. Sprinkle on about 1 tbs. Of olive oil and toss the spaghetti. Add a cup and a half of the tomato sauce to the spaghetti and toss. Serve four equal portions of spaghetti on 4 plates or pasta bowls. Top each serving of spaghetti with about 1/3 of a cup of sauce and serve.

7. Put a bowl of the grated cheese on the table and let everybody help themselves. "Bon Appetito"

NOTE: Tomato Sauce is what is known as a mother sauce. This Means that once you know how to make this "Base Sauce" that simply by adding one or more other ingredients, you can make another sauce. You can make many other sauces from this one base sauce, tomato sauce. If you sauté some mushrooms in a little olive with Garlic for about six minutes then add a couple cups of tomato sauce, that you already made, you now let simmer for a few minutes and you
have "Salsa Funghi," Mushroom Sauce to serve with whichever pasta you choose, Rigatoni, Spaghetti, or Farfalle would be good choices.
You can make Zucchini and Pepper Sauce simply my slicing and sautéing Sweet Peppers and Zucchini for a few minutes, then add some tomato sauce, simmer for

about 10 minutes and your Zucchini and Pepper Sauce is ready to be tossed with your pasta.

So whenever you make Tomato Sauce, don't just make for that night. Make double or triple. Save some in sealed containers in the refrigerator and some in freezer for later use on its own or to make another Sauce such as Mushroom or Zucchini and Peppers or a multitude of others. Tomato Sauce is "GREAT." It's easy to make, it's Most Economical and saves you a lot of MONEY, and if you make large batches it Saves You Time. "What More Could You Ask For!"

TOMATO SAUCE and Its OFFSPRING

As stated earlier, Tomato Sauce is what is known in the Culinary World as a Mother Sauce. Meaning that once you know this base sauce, you can make a hundred or two other sauces simply by adding different ingredients.

By adding different ingredients to a basic Tomato Sauce that you already have made, you can make; Pasta Puttanesca, Spaghetti with Broccoli, Rigatoni with Zucchini, Penne with Chicken, or a slew of other dishes. Listed below are just a few of the many.

"This Aggression will Not Stand!"

SPAGHETTI-O'S !!!

Spaghettti-O's? OK, what pure-blooded American kid hasn't eaten tons of SpaghettiOs over the years. Well some I guess, if they had parents that didn't like processed foods. Dude was actually too old to have eaten them as a child as Spaghetti-O's weren't invented and put on the market til 1965. No Dude discovered then in college when a college buddy of the Dude turned him on the wonderful little invention, round shaped pasta in tomato straight from the can. All you had to do was open the can, dump the Spaghetti-O's into a pan and heat them up, and "Voila," you had a tasty little meal ready in minutes. Kids just loved them, and they still do. They're a favorite of Stoners who are known to get serious munchies, which of-course includes our pal, The Dude. Dude has loved these tasty little suckers ever since his first encounter. He usually keeps a couple cans on hand for a fast, quick, and easy; lunch, dinner, or late-night munchies attack. However, one day, one of Dudes other buddies showed Dude how to make his own home-made Spaghetti-O's and with or without "Franks" (Hot Dogs) or Meatballs. Dude just loved the idea and makes himself a big-batch now and then, which once made, Dude can keep in a container in the fridge, to be heated-up at will in just a few minutes time. Great idea.

DUDES HOME-MADE SPAGHETTI-O'S

INGREDIENTS:

1 pound of Anelli Pasta (Little Ring Shaped Pasta)
5 cups of Tomato Sauce, recipe page 117
1 tablespoon Sugar, 2 tablespoons salt
6 Tbs. Ketchup
6 Hot Dogs, cut into ½" pieces
Grated Cheese (optional)

1. Heat tomato sauce with Hot-Dogs, Ketchup, and sugar in a small pot over low heat for 7 minutes.

2. Fill a 6 quart pot with water and 2 tablespoons salt. Bring to the boil.

3. Add Anelli (round pasta rings) to rapidly boiling water and cook according to directions on package.

4. When the Agnelli (pasta rings) are cooked, drain into colander, reserving a ¼ cup water. Put pasta back into the pot it cooked in. Add Olive Oil and mix. Add the tomato sauce with the Hot Dogs and mix.

5. Serve yourself a bowl of Spaghetti-O's & Franks and your guests if you have any. Place any leftover Spaghetti-O's in a container to be easily reheated for another quick and tasty meal in-no-time-flat!

Note: You can make the Spaghetti-O's without the Hot Dogs for original recipe, or you can add a batch of little DaFino Meatballs (recipe page 128, make them small) for *Spaghetti-O's & Meatballs*. Now that's just awesome. That's 3 meals in one.

RIGATONI with Zucchini & Yellow Squash

Dude says that this dish is a favorite of his many vegetarian friends. Of course, living in LA, California and what-not, Home of The Vegetarian. But hey, it's Dam Tasty in fact the Dude says. And though ole Duder is not a Vegetarian, he does like keeping his meat consumption to a minimum during the week, and actually eats meat just 3 to 4 times a week. It's a good balance of all food groups the Dude thinks. We agree as well!

1. To make Rigatoni with Zucchini and Yellow Squash, get 2 medium size Zucchini and one Yellow Squash of the same size. Wash these items, then slice them in about 1/8 inch slices. Sauté them in a little butter and olive oil as you do with the mushrooms in the previous recipe. Sauté over medium heat for about six minutes, stirring to make sure all the Zucchini and Squash slices are cooked on both sides. Season the slices with a little salt & Black Pepper to taste.

2. Cook, whichever Pasta you would like to use; Rigatoni, Spaghetti, Penne, etc.. Cook according to directions on package of pasta.

3. Add 1 ½ cups pre-made Tomato Sauce to pan with the Zucchini and Yellow Squash and cook over low heat for about 7 minutes until the tomato sauce is heated through.

4. Drain your cooked pasta in a colander. Add the drained pasta to pan with sauce and toss. Sprinkle in a ¼ cup of Grated Pecorino Romano Cheese when tossing pasta. Plate Pasta onto 4 individual plates or Pasta Bowls, serve and pass grated cheese. And as the Dude says, "Enjoy yourself!"

PUTTANESCA

The famous Neapolitan Pasta Dish of Spaghetti Puttanesca is tasty, quick, and easy to make. Anyone can do it. Named after the *Ladies of The Evening* (ladies who have a lot in common with Bunny) of the enchanting city of Napoli (Naples) in Southern Italy, who it is said, made this Quick and tasty dish, between clients, not a $1,000 clients, but maybe 1,000 Lire (Note: Lire is Italian Currency)

Pasta Puttanesca is quick and easy to make and a great dish for one of the Dudes 3 or 4 days a week he goes meatless. You simply sauté a some garlic in olive oil with chopped Anchovies, Capers, and Olives, add tomato sauce and cook while your pasta is boiling in a pot, "Quick & Easy." just like "The Girls" in Napoli.

1. Start by cleaning and slicing 3 cloves of garlic. Sauté the Garlic over low heat for about 3 minutes, being careful not to burn the garlic as burnt garlic leaves a bitter taste. Add; 6 Anchovy filets that have been finely chopped. Add 3 tablespoons of Capers that have been drained and washed. Add ¼ cup of Cured green or black Olives of your choice. We recommend Cerignola Olives.

2. Start cooking the pasta of your choice in boiling salted water. We like Spaghetti best with this sauce.

3. Sauté all these ingredients for two minutes over low heat. Add 2 cups tomato sauce and simmer over low heat for 6 minutes. Drain pasta, then toss in pan with

sauce. Serve and pass grated Pecorino Romano Cheese.
"Mangia"

MAUDE & DUDE WATCH "LOGJAMMIN"

Maude: *The story is Ludicrous!*
    You can imagine what happens next?

Dude: *He Fixes The Cable?*

DUDES SHROOMS SAUCE
Mushroom Sauce for Pasta

Yeah of course The Dude likes "Shrooms," all kinds, and this dish is dedicated to the kind he really loves. You know? Tony taught this one to Dude too. Once you have your basic tomato sauce made, go to the supermarket, your local grocer, Ralph's or a farm stand and get yourself some nice fresh mushrooms (Shrooms). You can use any kind of mushrooms for this sauce, the white Button Mushrooms that you can find in those little plastic baskets are most common and the kind the Dude uses most often, unless he is at a farm-stand and finds some more Exotic ones.

Ingredients:

1 pound dry or Fresh Pasta of your Choice
We suggest Spaghetti, Penne
or the Dudes favorite "Farfalle" (Butterflies)
1 ½ cups Tomato Sauce from previous Recipe
20 medium size Butter Mushrooms or any
Mushrooms you choose, sliced.
You may increase this amount if you like
Grated Parmigiano Reggiano Cheese to sprinkle over finished pasta
2 table spoons of butter, 1 tbs. olive oil
Salt & Pepper to taste

1. Sauté sliced mushrooms in pan with butter and olive oil over medium heat for 4 minutes, mushrooms with a wooden spoon, season with salt and pepper to taste.

2. Add tomato sauce to pan with mushrooms and heat Over a medium flame 2 minutes, then low flame for 4 minutes.

3. Cook pasta according to directions on box. Drain Pasta and add to pan with Mushroom Sauce.

4. Serve pasta amongst for plates and pass Grated Cheese to sprinkle on Pasta.

Dude says a couple nice variations on this Pasta with Mushroom Sauce would to be, instead of adding the above amount of tomato sauce you only add 3 tablespoons to the sautéed mushrooms, then add a ¼ cup of heavy cream, let it reduce a bit, then toss with pasta and serve. "It's Yummy," Dudes words.

Another variation would be to sauté the mushrooms in olive oil and butter with garlic, and don't add anything else, except maybe chopped fresh parsley if you have any on hand. And of course Dude says sprinkle on some good quality grated Parmesan Cheese.

And The Dude wants to point out at this juncture, do you see how easy it is, that once you have one base dish like Tomato Sauce for example, it's easy to make a number of other dishes simply by adding different ingredients?

Momma DaFino's Spaghetti & Meatballs

As all you Achievers know, the Dude didn't care too much for that creep DaFino. Following the Dude around all the time, making remarks about Dudes Special Lady Friend and what not, and suggesting to The Dude that they pool their resources, "Fuck-Off Da Fino," the Dude retorts to that.

A lot of good came out of that encounter between The Dude and DaFino though. "Certain Things Came to Light" about Bunny. "Who The Fuck are the Knutsen's?"

But even better than the Dude finding out about the Knutsen's and other things *coming to light*, New Shit, DaFino dropped a piece of paper with his mother's Meatball recipe on it. Dude picked it up, and the Dude doesn't have a problem using a recipe from someone he doesn't like, "two different things," and ole Duder can separate them, "No Problemo!"

It's a great Meatball recipe and illustrates the many uses of tomato sauce. You make a good sized batch of tomato sauce and as it's simmering, you mix up the ground meat and other ingredients to make the meatballs. You round off the Meatballs, then throw them into the sauce to cook for about 35 minutes, cook some Spaghetti and when it's done, "Voila" you've got yourself some fine Spaghetti & Meatballs. If you're smart, you'll make a double batch of both the tomato sauce and the Meatballs, so you'll have leftover Meatballs to make some nice "Meatball Parm Sandwiches" for the next day or two. "Tony Bag of

Donuts" suggested this to the Dude. It's a great idea, and something most Italians do every time they make a batch. It's an Italian-American ritual in fact, and Dude likes to do it too.

DUDES ENCOUNTER with Da FINO

Dude: Huh?

DaFino: *A Dick, Man! And let me tell you something, I dig your work. Playing one side against the other—in Bed with everybody – Fabulous Stuff Man.*

Dude: *I'm not a—ah, Fuck it, just stay away from my fucking Lady Friend, Man!*

DaFino: *Hey, hey, I'm not messing with your Special Lady –*

Dude: *She's not my Special Lady, she's my Fucking Lady Friend. I'm just helping her conceive man!*

Da Fino: *Maybe we can trade information, pool our resources?*

Dude: *FUCK Off DaFino !!!!*

MOMMA Da FINO'S
SECRET MEATBALL RECIPE

Ingredients:

1 lb. ground Beef
½ lb. ground Veal
½ Pound Ground Pork
4 Tbs. fresh Italian Parsley, chopped
1 minced onion
2 cloves garlic, minced
4 Tablespoons plain breadcrumbs
2 large eggs
Salt & pepper
½ cup grated Parmesan or Pecorino

Note: If you want, instead of this beef, pork and veal proportions, you can use just Beef (2 lbs.) or 1 lb. Ground Beef & 1 lb. Veal.

PREPARATION:

1. In a small bowl, break and beat eggs. Add breadcrumbs and let soak for 6 minutes.

2. In a large bowl, add all the remaining ingredients. Add eggs and mix well with your hands.

3. Shape meat mixture to form balls that are about 2 inches in diameter.

4. Coat the bottom of a cookie sheet or roasting pan with a thin film of olive oil. Cook Meatballs at 350 degrees for 10 minutes.

5. Make batch of Dudes Tomato Sauce (pg. 117). When the Sauce is finished cooking and the meatballs have partially cooked in the oven for 10 minutes, take meatballs out of oven and simmer for 35 in a the tomato sauce.

6. Serve Meatballs with Spaghetti for the Classic Italian American favorite Spaghetti and Meatballs or do as the Italians do, especially the Neapolitans and serve the sauce first with Spaghetti, Rigatoni, or ziti. Serve the Meatballs as the main course with a Salad or potatoes on the side.

GOOEY CHOP MEAT

This was a recipe from my Stepmother Joan. I gave this recipe to The Dude, and he absolutely loves it and for all the reasons that The Dude likes any of his favorite recipes. I think you know by now? Correctomundo! The name is "Crazy," Gooey Chop-Meat. I loved it, and that's what first got Dude interested in this dish as well, even before he ever tasted it. He heard about it, and with a name like "Gooey Chop Meat" and the description of the dish, The Dude just had to have it. Had to taste it, get the recipe, and now he makes it all the time. Dude makes about two batches a month. It's quick and easy. Tasty, it stores well, fills you up, and Dude gets about 14 plates per batch, the macaroni really stretches things far. Cost just about .50 cents a plate, ad that's Good by The Dude, "No Doubt."

Walter: *Is this your Homework Larry?*

Dude: *We're gonna Cut Your Dick Off Larry!*

GOOEY CHOP MEAT a RECIPE

"Wow.. This Gives Us a Great Idea!!! That Sounds Like Thee Greatest Title for a Horror Movie," called What Else, "GOOEY CHOP MEAT"

A Madman Bent on taking Over the World, Chops-Up people, turning them into Gooey Chop Meat making a Large Mass alla The BLOB... Remember Steve McQueen in it? What Do You Think? Crazy? It does Have Possibilities though..!!?? Just kidding!

This recipe will get you about 14 serving. You can eat some when you make it, refrigerate and or freeze the rest for later dates. Besides saving Money, this is one of those great "Time-Saving" recipes were by you take a little time to make a dish that will yield several more meals down the road. If you don't want to make as much, you can cut the recipe in half.

Walter: *Do you see what Happens Larry? Do you see What Happens, "When You F_ck a Stranger in the ASS?"*

GOOEY CHOP MEAT

Ingredients:

3 tablespoons Soy or vegetable oil
2 pound Ground Chuck or other Ground Beef
4 cloves of Garlic peeled and chopped
3 medium Onions, peeled and chopped
2 - 28 ounce cans chopped Tomatoes
½ tablespoon each of Kosher or Sea Salt

And Ground Black Pepper to taste
1 lb. Fusilli or Elbow Macaroni
or any pasta of your choice.
Dude prefers Fusilli for this recipe.
Use 1 pound of pasta for 3 or 4 people,
or ½ lb. for 2 people,   1 tablespoon Butter
¼ cup Grated Parmigiano or other cheese

Cooking Steps for GOOEY CHOP-MEAT

1. Put a 8 quart or other large pan on the stove top and add oil. Turn flame on to medium and heat 2 minutes. Add the chopped meat. Cook the chopped meat until it loses its raw color. Using a wooden spoon, break up the chopped meat as you cook it. It should take approximately ten minutes.

2. Add the garlic and onions and lower heat. Cook for 4 minutes.
3. Add tomatoes to pot. Raise heat to high and bring the tomatoes up to the boil, then lower the heat to low and cook for 25 minutes, periodically stirring with a wooden spoon.

4. After the sauce has been simmering for 20 minutes, put your pasta into a large pot of rapidly boiling salted water and Cook according to directions on package.

5. Drain the pasta. Put drained pasta back into the pot it cooked in. Spoon about 2 ½ cups of your sauce (Gooey Chop Meat) over the pasta. Add butter and mix.

6. Serve pasta on 4 plates, top with a little more sauce, and sprinkle on Grated Cheese.

Note: Put remaining Gooey Chop-Meat Sauce in air-tight containers in the frig, to heat up in about 10 minutes for a quick and tasty meal anytime of the day; lunch, dinner, Late-Night after Bowling, even for breakfast, It's All Good!"

If you don't want to cook pasta every time you reheat the leftovers, then cook 2 ½ pound of pasta, drain at when done. Add pasta back into the pot it cooked in, add a couple knobs of butter and all the sauce and mix. Eat some right then and there, then let the rest cool down before putting into containers in the frig.

When your gonna reheat, put whatever amount of pasta and sauce in a frying pan with about a ¼ cup of water, and heat over low heat for 6 minutes, stirring occasionally. Serve on a plate and don't forget the grated chees. Enjoy!

"Let me explain something to you, um, I'm the Dude, so that's what you call me. You know. That or uh, His Dudeness, Duder, or El Duderino, if you're not in to the whole brevity thing."

The Dude

KEEF'S FAVORITE SHEPHERD'S PIE

Yes *Keef*, as in Keith Richards of *The Rolling Stones*, the World's Greatest Rock-N-Roll Band *ever!* But you know that. This is the way Keith likes his Shepherds Pie, as does The Dude, and you will too. If it's good enough for Keef, it's good enough for the Dude, and you too. Abide!

INGREDIENTS:

3 pounds Potatoes, peeled and diced
1 tablespoon Butter
Salt & Pepper to taste
2 large Onions, chopped
2 pounds Ground Beef
2 large Carrots, grated
2 – 12 oz. cans Beef Broth
5 tablespoons water
1 tablespoon Cornstarch

1. Put potatoes in a large pot of salted water. Bring the water to the boil. Lower to a simmer and cook the potatoes until tender, about 8 minutes.

2. Drain potatoes once cooked.

3. Put cooked, drained potatoes in a large mixing bowl with the butter and season with salt and black pepper. Mash potatoes with a potato - masher or whip with an

electric mixer. If using a hand potato-masher, mash potatoes with masher, then mix with a wooden spoon until nicely whipped.

4. Heat a large frying-pan. Add 3 tablespoons of vegetable oil. Add ground-beef, cook over medium heat for 4 minutes. Add onions, continue cooking for minutes on high heat. Lower heat to low flame and cook 4 minutes more.

5. Add carrots and beef broth to pan. Mix cornstarch with water and add to pan. Cook over low flame for 8 minutes.

6. Add peas to pan, cook for 1 minute.

7. Pour Beef Mixture into a glass or ceramic baking dish. Evenly top beef with the mashed potatoes.

8. Bake in a 400 degree oven for 12 minutes, then place under the boiler until potatoes get nicely browned. Take care not to burn the potatoes once they are under the broiler.

9. Let cool slightly for 3 minutes and serve.

DUDE DOES RAMEN

Ramen, another Bedrock of "Dude Cookery." Ramen, quite a lot has been written, on the subject of Ramen, it's "One dam Great invention!" Hundreds of Millions of College Students over the years would agree. Ramen is also a favorite of those with limited means, and folks on a tight budget. Ramen wasn't around that much way back when our hero The Dude was going to college, so he didn't partake or Abide in "The Ramen" back then. You can *bet your sweet bippy* though, if Ramen was around and popular back then, Ramen would have been a major player in the Dudes College Diet along with canned Tuna and Spaghetti. The Dude however and for the past 15 years or so, has embraced Ramen and its varied uses in quite a big way.

Dude likes Ramen for its Thrifty Cost, Ease and Quickness of preparation. Dude usually whips up a Ramen Meal in about 10 minutes or less. Dude likes that. He also likes the versatility of Ramen and the cool packaging, and the Dude always keeps his cupboard packed Ramen that he gets at some large discount chain for about 6 packs for $1.00 .. Not Bad!

Dude says besides cans of Tuna, he always has Ramen, Eggs, and a can of Spam on hand, so if the frig and the rest of his cupboard is bare, he can whip up some dry seasoned Ramen, a couple slices of Spam and a Fried Egg or two and he's set 1, 2, Three!

COOKING RAMEN

Cooking Ramen Noodles is one of the simplest things one could ever wish to do, just follow the instructions on the back of the package. Actually there are two main ways to cook and serve Ramen Noodles. One way to cook Ramen Noodles is as a soup, which the way they are mainly intended. You place a couple cups of water into a pot. Bring the water to the boil, add the seasoning contents from the small flavor packet in the package. Add the noodles and let boil for 3 minutes. Your Ramen Noodle Soup is ready to eat. The Ramen is fine like this, but if you want a bit of a better meal, you can throw in and kind of fresh vegetable (Bok Choy, Broccoli, Carrots, etc..) that you have blanched beforehand. The second method is to cook the Ramen Noodles either in seasoned (from the flavor packet) or un-seasoned boiling water for three minutes, then draining the noodles in a Colander or Wire Basket and serving them dry. Once the noodles have been drained from the water or broth, you put them on a plate and season them to give them flavor. Many will reserve just a little water (2 tablespoons) and toss the water with about half of the seasonings from the flavor packet and they are ready to eat.

Dudes favorite way to prepare and eat Ramen Noodles is to cook the noodles in boiling water that has been seasoned with the whole contents of the flavor packet for 3 minutes, then draining the noodles to dry. The Dude places the noodles on a plate, sprinkles on a little salt, about a tablespoon of Sesame Oil ("Great Flavor"), then he hits it with one of his favorite Hot

Sauces such as; Sriracha, Louisiana Hot Sauce, Crystal, or Tabasco.

This preparation is absolutely delicious on its own. Dude eats it all the time; 2 or 3 times a week for a breakfast of Ramen and Eggs. The Dude often eats Ramen for lunch with one or two fried eggs that are seasoned with salt and pepper or with Maggie's Sauce, "Yum!" Besides eating Ramen Noodles for Breakfast or Lunch and occasionally dinner, The Dude often has a serving of Ramen in-between meals when he gets hungry. They are quick (just 3 minutes) and easy and just the right size. A portion of Ramen Noodles on their own with nothing else on the plate is enough to satisfy your hunger so that hungry feeling disappears and you are satisfied, and the portion size is not too much that it will ruin your meal that you plan on eating later and you will be able to eat that meal latter-on.

And we should point out here, being a Californian, The Dude and most of his fellow Californians really love Mexican and all Asian Cuisine Foods, and this is why Dude loves his Ramen with nice fresh green Asian vegetables, like Mustard Greens and especially Baby Bok Choy.

Along with eating dry Ramen Noodles on their own or with a little something on the side, you can have them with a piece of Kielbasa, a couple links of breakfast sausage, with Bacon, or one or two slices of fried Spam or Taylor Ham or any type of Ham you wish, even a Hot Dog or two will do.

So the Dudes really favorite way and one of the more nutritious ways to have his Ramen is when he buys a pound or two of Baby Bok Choy. The Dude simple blanches the Bok Choy in salted boiling water that he cooks the Ramen in. Once the water comes to the boil he throws in 2-3 heads of the Baby Bok Choy that has been washed and split in half. Let the Bok Choy cook in the water for about 2 ½ minutes, take them out of the water with a slotted spoon and place in a colander to let excess water drain. At this point you put your noodles and the contents of the flavor packet in the boiling water. Put the Bok Choy on the plate and sprinkle on a little salt and Sesame Oil.

Drain the Ramen Noodles from the water, place on the plate and season with salt, Sesame Oil, and Hot Sauce. "Voila! You have a quick (5-6 minutes), super economical meal that has tasty noodles and delicious nutritious Baby Bok Choy.

NOTE: You can use many different vegetables of your choice when making Ramen. Harder Green Vegetables such as Green Beans or Broccoli are best. You can also use the larger type of regular Bok Choy as well, but the baby type is preferred, and The Dude says it taste better and looks better on the plate to boot. Dude just loves it!

SPAM

Spam? Yes Spam! Here we go again, one of The Dudes all-time favorites from childhood. His Mom always had some in the cupboard where she would pull some out and serve it up with Scrambled or Fried Eggs if she was all out of fresh Polish Kielbasa, which the Lebowski's liked best, but the good old can of Spam was always there on hand whenever they needed it. Little Jeffrey really loved the taste and still does till this very day. And like his Mom, The Dude always has a can or two on hand right next to the "Tuna" in the cupboard. It's there if he has to make something good and tasty in a pinch. The Dude also always has eggs in the frig, so if he doesn't have anything else on hand, he always has of course the Tuna, a can or two of Spam, and Eggs, so he can always have a plate of tasty Fried Eggs and Spam. Yumm!!! It's a good thing to do, so make sure you do as the Dude and always have a can on hand; butter, canned Tuna, Eggs, and Spam, Mustard and Mayo and you'll never go hungry. Oh, yes, and you just know that along with Potato Chips and canned Tuna, The Dude subsisted on Spam as one of his main staple-foods during his illustrious college days of yore. Dudes Mom was always very kind and considerate during the Dudes college years, sending many "Care Packages" to her son Jeffrey. The care packages always filled with cans of Tuna, Spam, Spaghetti, Jars of Tomato Sauce, Twinkies, and Ring Dings. What a nice Mom that Mrs. Lebowski was! Still is!

Yes "SPAM?" Spam is somewhat of a social food phenomenon of the U.S., especially in the great state of

Hawaii where it is it is as Hawaiian as Apple Pie is American.

Spam is a pork based Ham-Type product that was developed during World War II to help to feed both Soldiers and civilians during the Second World War.

Spam the brand is not all that economical compared to other meats or meat product. However, used in the proper manner with other ingredient and compared to going out to eat a Breakfast or Lunch, the use of Spam or other similar product can prove to be quite inexpensive and a great saver of Money, something the Dude always keeps in mind when shopping and cooking food. The price per pound of Spam does make it a bit expensive compared to buying a larger piece of real ham or a fresh piece of pork. The latest price we've seen was $3.59 for a 12 oz. can.

There are other products that are almost the same as Spam and cost far less, and The Dude usually buys a brand from Holland that you can get in most markets in Chinatown in LA or New York for $1.59 for the same 12 oz. can. A savings of $2.00, that's quite good.

One of the best meals to make from Spam and one of the Dudes personal favorites, is to slice and fry two pieces of *Spam* and serve with either dry-seasoned Ramen Noodles and or two Fried Eggs.

SPAM DISHES

So as the Dude has already pointed out, simply frying up some Spam and a couple eggs is his favorite of all Spam-Dishes. Fried Eggs or Scramble, depending on The Dudes mood, are all good for The Dude. Also pretty much the same thing but on a roll is a Spam and Egg Sandwich. You get yourself a nice Hard Roll (or Bread), fry up a couple slices of Spam and fry or scramble 1 or 2 eggs, plop them on your roll or between two slices of bread and "Voila" you've got yourself a tasty Duder Spam and Egg Sandwich. And yes if you want to Guild the Lilly as they say, yes you can throw on a slice of cheese. Yumm!!!

Supposedly there are tons of ways to cook and utilize Spam. There are books written on the subject, Booklets anyway. Dude knows this, but he likes to keep it simple and the few Spam preparations he makes are so tasty and satisfying, the Dude doesn't see any reason to mess with a whole bunch of others. So the Dude eats the *Spam* in two different ways, either as is in the just mention sandwich, simply 2 slices of Fried Spam with 2 eggs, or he throws Ramen into the mix, in which he'll have on a plate, a portion of Ramen seasoned with salt, pepper, and Sesame Oil, 1 Fried Egg, and a slice or two of fried Spam. That's it, nice, simply, and easy, and of course, tasty as can be. Walter likes em too, the Spam in the can reminds Walter of his days in "Nam," (Vietnam) and the K-Rations the soldiers were given to eat in the field.

RAMEN & SPAM alla DUDERINO

Dude invented this tasty little dish one day when he was hungry for mid-afternoon lunch. He made it with some favorites that he always has on hand; Eggs, Spam, Peas, & Ramen Noodles of course. It's upper quick (12 minutes) to make and tasty as can be, you know The Dude wouldn't have it any other way.

1 package Ramen Noodles,1 Extra Large Egg
2 slices Spam, ¼ cup frozen Peas
3 tablespoons Olive Oil, Salt & Black Pepper
¼ teaspoon Maggi's Sauce, 2 tablespoons Sesame Oil
Hot Sauce, optional

1. Cook Spam in olive in a frying pan, 2 minutes on each side until nicely browned over medium heat.

2. Remove Spam from pan and set aside. Beat an egg in a small bowl with a pinch of salt & pepper and cook in the pan the spam cooked in until eggs are cooked through.

3. Cook Ramen in boiling water according directions on pack-age. Cut Spam into small squares and add to pan. Add peas to pan and cook 1 minute. Turn heat off. Drain Ramen from water and add to pan. Add Maggi's Sauce and Sesame Oil to pan. Season with salt & pepper to taste, mix all ingredients and serve.

TAYLOR HAM

PS.. There's another product the Dude wants you to know about that he picked up from some friends when the Dude was on The Speed of Sound Tour with those "Assholes" from *Metalica*. It's Taylor Ham a.k.a. Taylor Pork Roll. The stuff is real Yummy and just as Dudes friends in Hawaii love their Spam more than others around the country, his friends in Jersey are nuts for this stuff. Dude says they have good reason to be, the stuff is "Tasty as hell!"

Taylor Ham is used in the same ways you would use Spam, and Taylor Ham and Egg Sandwiches in Jersey are all the rage, Dude says "They're The BOMB" !!! And "Yes," Taylor Ham is big with our friends in Philly too.

DUDES TAYLOR HAM & EGG SANDWICHES

Ingredients:
2 slices of Taylor Ham
1 or 2 Extra Large Eggs
1 fresh Hard Roll

Slice your roll in half. Fry the Taylor Ham. Remove from pan and place on bottom half of the roll. Scramble or fry the egg, season with salt and pepper. Place in roll with the Taylor Ham and Enjoy yourself. Add a slice or 2 or Swiss or Cheddar and you've got a Taylor Ham Egg and Cheese Sandwich. It's The BOMB!!!!

BURGERS & DOGS

What's more American than Hamburgers and Hot Dogs? Answer, Nothing! Not even Apple Pie! Doesn't even come close. Americans probably eat 100 times more Burgers than Apple Pie. This is true of the beloved Hot Dog too, and the reasons The Dude Loves both.

Hot Dogs are one of the easiest things you can ever want to make, and The Dude, Walter, Donny, and Brandt all love them. Bunny too, "especially Bunny." Get it? Bunny likes Hot Dogs. "That Slut! She Kidnapped herself! You said it yourself Dude."

Donny, as we all know really loves a good In-N-Out Burger, and Carneys too and Chili Dogs at Pinks. Dude most of the time goes out for a Burger, but he likes makin em at home too. But when it comes to Chili Dogs, Dude prefers them at home, especially since he makes his famous Cowboy Chili once or twice a month and often has Chili on hand. So the Dude besides making Burritos and Tacos with the Chili, he always makes a good number of Chili Dogs too.

And when Dude makes his famed Chili he usually invites Walter and Donny over for a couple Dogs before they head over to the Lanes. Walter and Donny do appreciate The Dudes tasty Chili Dogs before or after a good night of throwing Gutters but hopefully mostly Strikes. "Fwehh I'm on fire tonight. Mark it Dude," (says Donny after throwing a Strike). It's Good Old Fashion American Fun, Chili Dogs, Beer, and Bowling.

Yes Hamburgers and Hot Dogs, Frankfurters, Weenies, or simply Dogs. Millions of each are eaten every day. They are part of the American Fabric, Dudes World, mine and yours, Achievers too.

Cooking them? The Hot Dogs? The Easiest way is to boil them. You can cook them in a frying pan with a little oil, which browns them nicely and is super easy. This is the way Dude most often does them, but he'll occasionally boil them too, especially when he's gonna throw on some Cowboy Chili and Cheese. What's better than that?

Now the Burger, that's a little more complicated. You're are dealing with raw meat here. Ground raw meat at that, and you need to cook the Burger according to the way you like them; rare, medium, well done, whatever? A Hot Dog is already cooked and all you're doing is heating it up and adding Chili or "What Not."

The single most important thing with a Burger is that the meat is fresh! "Super Fresh" at that, Dude says. What kind of meat? Well chopped meat, Ground Beef. Ground Chuck or ground Sirloin is most popular. And you usually want to get ground beef that has a fat content of between 15 and 20% fat. Twenty percent fat is better for tastier juicy Burgers.

Dude wants you to know the most important thing after freshness when it comes to Burgers is to keep it simple. Don't mix flavorings like spices and other things into the meat. The only seasonings you need when making a Burger is Salt & Black Pepper on the outside of the beef patty. After the Burgers are cooked, you can add; Mustard, Ketchup, slice raw or sautéed onion, maybe sliced tomato, and lettuce. And of course, a slice or two of Cheese thrown on top is always great. Being a Californian, Dude likes to make a California Burger at times, with a slice of ripe Tomato and

Avocado, or a New Mexican, with some good Green Chili Sauce.

But Dudes favorite is a plain ole Cheeseburger or, you guessed it, Chili Cheeseburger now and then, though most often Dude reserves the Chili for the Dogs. And yes, Bacon is always good too. After these aforementioned items, if you want more, then you are going overboard and killing a good thing. Keep it simple Dude says. You want to taste of the Beef, and embellished by either a little mustard, Ketchup, onion, and maybe lettuce and tomato, yes, The California Burger, it's okay.

Burger Size? Dude doesn't like burgers that are too thick as some like them. The best size is a bit more than a half-inch thick and round to fit a Burger Bun perfectly or just slightly going out past the bun, just a little. And the best Burgers are cooked on a Flat Top surface in their own fat. Forget about cooking on a hot grill that leaves hard burnt surfaces and you lose the tasty fat when in falls through the grill slots. That's lost forever! So Sad!

At home, The Dude says cooking your burgers simply in a frying pan with a bit of oil added in, is the best and tastiest way to go.

And when serving your burgers at home, you might want to serve some nice pickle spears on the side, along with some Potato Chips. That's The Dudes favorite way, with some Chips and a couple Sour Pickle Spears on the side. Yumm!!! Make em, Enjoy em, and always Abide, says our hero The Dude.

"You Can Find Your Way Across the
Country Using BURGER JOINTS
the Way a Navigator Uses Stars."

Charles Kuralt

DUDE BURGER

Dude says this is Thee Classic Burger. His rendition of an In-N-Out Double-Double that he and Donny developed follows this one (The Dude Burger). As for taste and what not, Dude likes them both. When he's experimenting a little; throwing on some Green Chili, Bacon, or Cowboy Chili, Dude uses this one. Dude says, try em both. You'll like.

INGREDIENTS for 4 DUDE BURGERS:

1 ¼ Lb. Fresh Good Quality Ground Beef (15-20% fat)
Salt & Pepper
4 or 8 slices good quality American or Cheddar Cheese
4 Hamburger Buns
2 tablespoons vegetable oil
Ketchup (Heinz is the Best)

OPTIONAL INGREDIENTS:

Sliced raw Onion or sautéed Onions,
Bacon, Mustard, Pickles, Lettuce, Tomato

DUDE BURGER COOKING INSTRUCTION:

1. Divide the Ground Beef into 4 equal parts. Shape Beef into Patties about ½ inch thick.

2. Heat a frying pan (Skillet) over medium heat for 3 minutes. Add oil, and heat 15 seconds. Turn flame up to high. Add raw beef patties. Cook 2 minutes. Season burgers with Salt & Pepper. Turn heat down to medium, cook for two minutes..

3. Turn heat back up to high. Turn burgers over to other side. Cook for two minutes until Burgers are about medium well, which is the Best way to cook a burger. Cook a little less if you want a medium Burger and less still if you want your cooked Burger Medium Rare.

BURGER NOTES: To cook your Burgers on the back-yard grill, it usually takes about 6 minutes to cook a Half-Inch Thick Burger depending on the heat of the grill, about 4 minutes on the first side and then you turn the burger over and cook it two three minutes on the second side.

Also, make sure not to make the common era of flipping your burger several time. You need to flip it once to get the best results. Yes, just once. That's it, 1 Tim, and as Roberto Duran would say, "No Mas!"

A good trick for you to know, which most home cooks do not know is that you can use a knife to poke into the center of the burger to see how much it is cooked in the center. If you look into the center and see it is rarer than you would like it to be cooked, then you will know that you have a few more minutes to cook it. This is a great trick to know for all cooking, so get in the habit of doing it as it is one of the greatest pieces of cooking knowledge you'll ever get. This is particularly good method to use when cooking chicken or turkey to look inside to see if the bird is cooked through or if it is still a little raw and you'll need to cook it more.

As we have laid out instructions to cook a Burger on an outdoor grill as many like to cook them this way. We will reiterate that personally, we feel cooking a Burger cooked in a pan or a Flat-Top-Grill where the Burger can cook in its own fat is the Best way. It gives the burger more flavor, and the burger gets evenly browned, but if you want to cook the burgers on an outdoor grill, that's your choice and your prerogative as the Stranger would say.

Note: The above recipe is for 4 Dude Burgers. If you want just one then just use a ¼ of the amount of ground beef, Hamburger Buns, and Cheese. To make 2 Burgers, cut the ingredient amounts in half.

IN-N-OUT BURGER

Walter: He lives in North Hollywood on Radford near the In-N-Out Burger.

Dude: Uh, the In-N-Out Burger is on Camrose.

Walter: Near the In-N-Out Burger. The—

Donny: Those are good Burgers Walter.

Walter: Shut the Fuck Up Donny.

Walter: Anyway, we'll go over there after the uh…
We'll brace the kid, should be a push over…

Donny: We'll be near the In-N-Out Burger.

Walter: SHUT THE FUCK UP DONNY !!!

Donny: In-N-Out.

Dude: Hey, shhh shhh man.

Walter: We'll get some Burgers, some Beers,
have a few Laughs.
Are troubles are over Dude.

Re-ENACTMENT of "THE DOUBLE-DOUBLE"

The In-N-Out "Double-Double" is much loved and preferred of the wonders of In-N-Out-Dom. A Double Double is; Two Beef Patties, Two Slices of Cheese, lettuce, a slice of Tomato, and In-N-Out Special Sauce on a toasted bun. Donny in a couple years of trial and era, making them and going back and forth to the In-N-Out on "Camrose" making taste comparisons of the In-N-Out Double-Double to Donny's.

Donny did his research, with the help of The Dude and Walter of course. He made his tweaks. They wrote their recipe, instructions and advice down for their friends and all "The Achievers" of the World to have. And here it is after years of painstaking research and experimentation, The Dude & Donny Double-Double reenactment recipe. Make it, Eat it, Enjoy It and Abide!

"SHUT THE FUCK UP DONNY" !!!

DUDE and DONNY'S
Reenacted DOUBLE-DOUBLE

INGREDIENTS:

1 good quality Hamburger Bun
6 oz. Fresh Best Quality Ground Beef
Salt & ground Black Pepper
1 tablespoon Thousand Island Dressing
1 slice fresh Ripe Tomato
2 Slices Real Yellow American Cheese
1 piece Boston Lettuce
1 thin slice of Onion

INSTRUCTIONS: Per Dude and Donny

1. Divide ground Beef into 2 equal portions. Shape into two Hamburger Patties.

2. Heat a small frying pan on medium heat flame.

3. Toast Bun in pan. Remove to the side.

4. Season each side of each burger patty with Salt and Pepper to taste.

5. Place burger patties in pan and cook over medium to high flame for 3 minutes.

6. Flip Burger to other side and continue cooking for 2-3 minutes more.

ASSEMBLAGE

Got Any Kahlua?

1. Place bottom part of Bun on a plate.

2. Spread 100 Islands Dressing on Bun.

3. Add Tomato slice, then Lettuce.

4. Place 1 Beef Patty on top and 1 slice of Cheese on this 1st Beef Patty.

5. Lay on the slice of Onion, then 2nd Beef Patty with 2nd slice Cheese. Top with Bun. You're set.

You've now got yourself a nice Re-Creation of the famed In-N-Out Double-Double. Some might ask, "Why the Hell would you want to go through all the trouble to make a copy of this tasty treat The Double-Double?" Especially when they are so cheap, and there's nothing better than the original?

Well my friends. Number 1, there happens to be many fans of The Dude and The Double-Double all across "This Great Country of Ours" as the Cowboy Stranger would say. And guess what, In-N-Out is only on the West Coast. There are Millions of unfortunates all across the country who can not go out and get themselves one of these tasty treats, "The Double-Double." They do not have an In-N-Out nearby. They cannot get themselves an In-N-Out at all, so they must create. And the Dude and Donny have been good enough to go through much trouble, experimentation, and research to come up with a pretty good version to make "All Over this Great Country of Ours" on The East Coast, Down South, The Mid West, and yes even in the West and in LA as the Dude and Donny do once and a while do.

Well, I'll say it right here and now. Thank You Donny, and Thank You Dude for all your great efforts, "It's much appreciated," says The Cowboy and all the those good, loyal, honest "Achievers" out there, wherever they may be, and that's all across the land.

Eat, Drink, Abide!

Monti: *Dude, tomorrow's already the 10th.*

Dude: *Far Out--- Oh--Uh, OK.*

Monti: *Just slip the Rent under my door.*

Dude: *Uhh? Ahh, OK.*

DOGS

Hot Diggity Dog! Hot Dogs? Dude likes his more or less one way most of the time, and that's The Dudes favored Chili Cheese Dog with Dudes famous Cowboy Chili. All you gotta do is either boil, grill on an outdoor grill or pan-fry in a pan a couple good quality Hot Dogs, heat up some Chili, put a Hot Dog in a Bun, slather on some Chili, top with some grated Cheddar or American Cheese and enjoy!

Dude likes to stop at Carney's or Pinks every once and a while, but other than these two joints Dude would rather have a Coney (other name for Chili Dog) at home with his own home-made Cowboy Chili.

DUDES CHILI DOGS

2 Hot Dogs (whatever is your favorite)
2 Hot Dog Rolls
5 tablespoons Dudes Cowboy Chili (heated)
Cheddar or Yellow American Cheese (optional)

1. Heat a frying pan over medium heat. Open Hot Dog buns and place in pan, heat and toast buns. Remove from pan and keep on the side.

2. Sauté Hot Dogs in pan with vegetable oil over medium heat. Cook Hot Dogs until all sides are lightly browned. Fill buns with Hot Dogs, top with Chili, and top with Cheese if using. Serve, eat, and enjoy.

BERKHOLTZER'S KRAUT

Walter: *"I told that "Fucking Kraut" at the league office that I don't Fuckin Roll on Shabbos --- What's his name?"*

Donny: *"Berkholtzer ... But he already posted it."*

Walter: *"Well he can Fucking Un-Post It!"*

Note: "KRAUT" is a German word recorded in English from 1918 onwards as a derogatory term for a German person, particularly a German Soldier during World War I and World War II. Germans were and still are called Kraut in slang terminology, after Sauerkraut. Kraut is a German language synonym for Sauerkraut.

Ingredients:

8 ounces Franks Kraut (Sauerkraut) or other quality brand, in a can jar, or bag. Type in jar or bag preferred.
2 tablespoons vegetable oil, 1 tablespoon Butter
Ground Black Pepper
1 teaspoon Caraway Seeds (optional)

1. Drain Sauerkraut in strainer to remove as much water as possible.

2. Place oil in frying-pan and heat over medium heat for 1 minute. Add Sauerkraut.

3. Add butter, Black Pepper, and Caraway Seeds if using. Cook over medium heat for 5 minutes, stirring occasionally. Serve on Hot Dogs.

This way of cooking Sauerkraut, is a bit tastier than the normal way of emptying the contents of a can, jar, or bag of Sauerkraut into a pan with its water, heating it up and serving. This manner of cooking the Sauerkraut used by Berkholtzer and others (including Walter) is much tastier than just cooking it in water. Draining the Sauerkraut and slightly browning it in vegetable oil and butter, gives a slight caramelization to the Kraut, giving it a richer more satisfying flavor to top your Frankfurter (Hot Dog) with.

NIHILIST PIGS IN A BLANKET

Waitress: *"What can I get you?"*

Nihilist 1: *"I'll have Lingonberry Pancakes."*

Nihilist 2: *"Lingonberry Pancakes."*

Nihilist 3: *"Pigs in A Blanket."*

INGREDIENTS:

24 Cocktail Hot Dogs or 8 regular size Hot Dogs cut into three pieces each
12 sliced Bacon cut in half
3 packs Pillsbury Crescent Rolls

1. Place Bacon on baking pan and cook in a 350 Degree oven for 6 minutes. Do not make too crisp.

2. When the Bacon has cooled, wrap each Mini Dog in a piece of Bacon, then wrap the Bacon wrapped Hot Dog inside of a piece of Crescent Dough.

3. Place on a cookie-pan and bake in 320 degree oven and bake for 10-12 minutes until dough is slightly golden brown.

4. Let cool for 4 minutes and serve.
These little Cocktail Treats are great at a Cocktail Party with White Russians and "What-Not," or something to munch on as you watch "The Big Lebowski" for your 100th time. Abide! For a real great party line-up, serve; White Russians, Bunny's Porno Punch, Pigs in a he Blanket, and The Dudes Crazy Wings, and maybe a

little of Guacamole and Chips, "Dudes Way." Your friends will love it, and your party should be a sure-fire success. Throw on a DVD or the Big Lebowski Soundtrack and you're in for some good times. Enjoy.

Nihilist 2: *His Girlfriend gave up Her TOE..*

Nihilist 3: *She thought we'd be getting a Million Dollars*

Nihilist 2: *Iss not fair !!!*

DUDE ABIDES BBQ CHICKEN

Dude likes makin Barbecued Chicken every now and then, especially in the Summer as it then reminds the Dude of his childhood and his mom making it for little Jeffrey in pre Dude America. Dude says, he has always loved the taste, as a boy, now, and always, and he says he's got a real easy way to make it. Dude says, you make it when chicken is on sale, not when it's not. Remember one of Dudes rules, "never pay full retail!" Some of you already know this, if not, do Abide by. Dude always does, and for it, he's got more ready cash, cash for Bowling, W_ _d, driving around, a-little-of-this-a-little-of-that, "you know."

Yes, buy the chicken when it's on sale, .79 to .99 cents a pound, something like that, not when it's $1.99 or $2.49, OK? Likewise with the Barbecue Sauce. What do you do? Right, buy a bottle or 2 when it's on sale. Often times you can find a good bottle of barbecue sauce on sale for as low as .99 cents, as compared to $1.99, $2.99. $3.99 or more.

Dudes method of making barbecued chicken is super simple, and the recipe follows. Dude says serve it with Potato Salad, Macaroni Salad, or Corn on The Cobb on the side. The combination just can't be beat. Abide!

DUDES ABIDING BBQ CHICKEN

INGREDIENTS:

3 pounds Chicken Parts
(Dude likes thighs and Wings Best)
4 tablespoons vegetable oil
Salt & Black Pepper to taste
1 bottle of Barbecue Sauce, your favorite
that was on sale

1. Pre-heat oven to 400 degrees.

2. Place chicken in a large baking pan that is big enough to hold all of the chicken piece without crowding.

3. Add oil and coat the chicken with the oil. Turn all the chicken pieces skin side down. Season all the chicken with salt & pepper. Turn all chicken so the skin side is up. Season the skin side of all the chicken with salt & pepper to taste.

4. Place chicken in oven and cook at 400 degrees for 10 minutes.

5. Lower oven to 350. Turn chicken over, skin side down, and cook chicken for 10 minutes.

6. Brush the chicken with barbecue sauce. Turn chicken over to skin side up and brush barbecue sauce on to the skin side of the chicken pieces. Cook for 8 minutes at 350 degrees.

7. Remove chicken from oven. Let set 7 minutes before serving. Serve with Corn on The Cobb, potato salad or whatever you little heart desires. It's Dude Abides BBQ Chicken, so, "Enjoy!"

BUFFALO CHICKEN WINGS

Buffalo Chicken Wings, you know the Dude loves them. They go hand and hand with Dudes favorite past time, "Bowling." These little suckers are tasty as Hell, and good reason millions of them are consumed in the U.S. on a daily basis. They're Tasty and Iconic-ally American. People just *Love Em*, "Pure and Simple" says the Dude.

DUDE STYLE
BUFFALO CHICKEN WINGS

2 lbs. Chicken Wings
½ cup vegetable oil, 1/3 stick Margarine or Butter
Black Pepper and Salt
2 ½ tablespoons Hot Sauce (Tabasco, Frank's, etc.)

1. Prep the wings by cutting off the tip and discarding them, then cut the Wing in half at joint to make 2 pieces.

2. Season Chicken Wings with Salt & Black Pepper.

3. Heat vegetable oil in a large frying –pan. Cook the Wings in batches, probably 3 batches depending on how many wings you have and how big your pan is.

4. Cook the wings about 4 minutes on each side over medium heat.
5. Place the wings in a large baking pan. Set in the oven at 350 degrees for 20 minutes

6. Melt Butter or Margarine in a small pot.

7. Remove all oil from pan.

8. Place Wings in a large bowl with melted butter or margarine and Hot Sauce, mix all thoroughly, coating all the wings.

BLUE CHEESE DIP

1 cup Mayonnaise
4 oz. crumbled Blue Cheese
2 tablespoons White Vinegar, Black Pepper
¼ cup Heavy Cream

1. In a large bowl, mix all ingredients except Heavy Cream.

2. Slowly add Heavy Cream mixing with a wooden spoon until dressing is of the consistency you desire.

Slice Celery into 3 inch sticks. Serve Buffalo Wings with Celery Sticks and Blue Cheese Dressing, Abide and Enjoy!

DUDES CRAZY WINGS

The Dude really loves his Chicken Wings, the Buffalo type, or plainly roasted with salt & pepper and this way, created by the Dude himself, in which the Dude seasons the wings with Honey, Mustard, and Soy Sauce, and The Dude calls them "Crazy Wings," cause they are, *Crazy Good*! Two bonuses with this Dude created dish, they're super tasty and real easy to make, and Great for Parties.

INGREDIENTS:

2 lb. Chicken Wings
Salt and ground Black Pepper
6 tablespoons Dijon or Brown Mustard
6 tablespoons Canola or Corn Oil
6 Tablespoons Honey, 4 tablespoons Soy Sauce
2 tablespoons Sriracha Sauce or other Garlic
Red Pepper Sauce

1. Prep the Chicken Wings by cutting off the inedible Tip. The wing is now in a letter "V" shape. Cut in the middle at the joint, cutting the wings into two pieces. Pre heat oven to 400 degrees.

2. Place all the wings in the largest baking pan you or 2 pans if you don't have one large one to hold all the wings.
3. Add oil of choice, Salt & Black Pepper to thoroughly coat all the wings with the oil, Salt & Pepper.

4. Cook wings at 400 degrees for 10 minutes. Turn heat down to 350 degrees and continue cooking the wings for about 17 minutes.

5. Take wings out of oven and add the soy sauce, Honey, Mustard, and Sriracha Sauce to pan with Wings. Mix all ingredients so the Wings get evenly coated.

6. Put the wings back in oven and cook for seven minutes. Take Wings out of oven. Let cool about 5 minutes. Place on a platter, serve, and Enjoy.

The Dude developed this recipe one day cause Ralph's was having a sale on Chicken Wings. The Dude got a whole big tray of wings real cheap and brought them home. Dude looked in his cupboard and pulled out a jar of honey, Soy Sauce, a bottle of Sriracha Sauce, and some Dijon Mustard. Dude figured these flavors would taste pretty dam good on the Chicken Wings. He was right. That day, The Dudes "Crazy Wings" were born. They are dam tasty, Dude thinks you will agree. He's pretty proud of this invention, as he should be. They're Dam Good. Make them, Eat them, Love them, and share them with Friends and other Achievers, and everyone will just love you. The Dude too! Abide.

THE DUDE DOES STEAK

Steak? The Dude? The Dude and Steak? The Dude and Steak, what does the Dude like? Does he like steak? Loves it? What? Of course he likes Steak. Dude like many American males loves himself a good juicy steak every now and then. He doesn't eat them all that often as they are a bit expensive, and as we all know the Dude is unemployed, "Are You Employed Sir?" Dude, "What day is this? Is this--- a--a week day?"

Yes steaks are more expensive than many a food item, and the Dude prefers to more often invest his money on ground beef most of the time to make his killer Cowboy Chili, Dudes Crazy Wings, or Gooey Chop Meat. For the money the Dude spends on a steak to get just one meal, he can buy chopped meat and all the other ingredients to make a batch of Chili big enough to get about 24 servings out, as a opposed to just a one serving meal. A good quality Sirloin Steak usually cost the Dude about $10.00. That's for one meal. He gets 24 meals from the Chili. If he had 24 Steaks, it would cost the Dude about $240 as opposed to just $10.00 for 24 meals based on Dudes Chili. Do you get the Dudes point and see his reasoning?

All this being said, The Dude like most American men does enjoy himself a nice juicy Sirloin Steak every-now-and-then, Walter does even more so. The Dudes view and "Philosophy on Steak" is that he treats it as a "Special Treat" and usually has one just 4 to 6 times a year. If you eat something all the time, it doesn't seem so special. Things like Caviar, Foe Gras, White Truffles are very expensive luxury items, kind of prohibitively expensive and mostly for the "Rich" (The Other Lebowski *"The Big Lebowski"*). White Truffles cost about $1,000 a pound. Yes I said $1,000 a pound. We think Caviar is priced somewhere about the same.

Anyway Steak isn't cheap, but a lot cheaper than Caviar or White Truffle. Steak, it's an "affordable luxury" should we say. Dude'll bet half the Achievers in the World don't even know what the Hell a White Truffle is. They don't even give a F_ck! No it's nothing like a "White Russian."

Yes, Steak you say! And luxury foods, Dude can't afford Caviar. He doesn't even like the stuff, and doesn't understand how any one in their right mind would pay a thousand dollars a pound for the stuff. "Now Weed," on the other hand? Anyway Dude like many people treat a serious Sirloin Steak as a "Special Treat," and an affordable luxury, and that though a bit expensive, not too expensive or out of the realm of the Dudes limited means. The Dude can afford a good Steak every-now-and-then and it makes him feel good to eat one. For in the Blue Collar Middle Class, Steak is a Luxury, an affordable one.

No, the Dude doesn't eat steak all the time. He makes a Steak maybe once every two to three months or so. There are actually some out there who might eat steak twice a week, 6 times a month anyway. Dude is not into eating steak twice a week, not even twice a month. He feels if you eat Steak too often, it's not quite so special, The Dude says, and The Dude always wants to keep his Steak Special, a *Special Treat*. We hear the Big Lebowski eats Steak twice a week, "it Figures." Dude will keep it as Special Treat, not a twice weekly thing. How bout you?

Walter: *We are Sympathizing here Dude ..*

Dude: *Fuck Sympathy. I don't need sympathy. I need my "FUCKING JOHNSON" !!!*

Donny: *What do you need "that" for Dude ?*

COOKING a STEAK...
"DUDES WAY"

Dude says when you're cooking yourself a Steak, keep it simple. First off you gotta get yourself a good steak, and it should be "Prime" for best flavor and not "Choice" which without question is inferior and doesn't taste nearly as good. Seriously! That "Choice Steak" may look just as good as the "Prime" but it isn't, there's a reason the Prime Steak cost 50% or more than the choice one, it's way better. Trust Ole Duder on this one. See a Prime Steak cost quite a bit more than the Choice Steak. Dude could buy Choice Steaks and eat steak more often, but it wouldn't taste nearly as good. Dude would rather eat a delicious Prime Steak that is at the Top of its Game in tastiness, than to eat steak twice as much but they're not really that tasty. Catch the Dudes drift Donny?

INGREDIENTS:

1 "PRIME" SIRLOIN STEAK 10 to 14 ounces
Ground Black Pepper and Kosher or Sea Salt
Butter
Vegetable Oil

1. Season your Steak with Salt and Pepper on both Sides.

2. Heat a frying pan over high heat for 3 minutes.

3. Put 2 tablespoons of oil in pan. Heat oil for 10 seconds, then add steak to pan. Medium Rare is the best temperature for a steak.

4. It's going to depend how thick your steak is for its cooking time. A good trick in cooking your steak is periodically peaking inside the steak by making a slit with a sharp thin knife and looking in the middle of the steak.

5. Cook your steak over high heat for three minutes, lower the heat to medium and cook two minutes more. Raise the heat to high and flip your Steak over to the other side.

6. Cook the steak for two minutes, then cut and look inside to the middle of the steak to see if you want to take the steak off the fire, or if you want to cook it for 2, 3, or 4 minutes more depending on if you want your steak Medium Rare, Medium, or Well Done.

7. When the Steak is done. Put it on a plate with whatever type potato or vegetable you'd like.

8. Take a half-teaspoon of butter and spread it over your Steak and add a little more Salt and Pepper if you'd like. Enjoy!

LONDON BROIL...The Poor Man's Steak

*"the Perfect Steak for The Dude
and All you Achievers too!"*

London Broil was once a All-American Classic that was "Uber Popular in the 50's, 1960s and 70's, the Dude's Mom used to make it as a special treat maybe twice a month. They almost never ate Sirloin Steak in the Lebowski Household when young Jeffrey (The Dude) was growing up. Sirloin Steak was usually reserved for grown men. Businessmen (The Big Lebowski) at business meetings in a Steak House or just a few guys getting together on guys night out and going out for a Steak once or twice a year. No, the Lebowski's never ate Sirloins Steaks, but Mrs. Lebowski did quite often make London Broil, and a Dam tasty one at that. Young Jeffrey watched. He learned.

So why you say was London Broil so popular back then? Why? Well, it's cheap and fairly tasty. We say fairly tasty, as it can be quite good, but definitely not as good as a juicy Sirloin or Rib Eye Steak, which have much higher fat contents making for juicier, more tender cuts of meat. However, they are much more expensive, double to triple the price per pound of the much cheaper Flank Steak known all over America as London Broil. And Mrs. Lebowski like that name "London Broil." It sounded "Fancy." It does, and she like that. Hey those meat market beef pushing ranchers and what not are no dummies. They put a fancy name on a lesser cut of meat and dam if it doesn't sell like Hot-Cakes.

London Broils popularity is attributed to the fact that multitudes of Americans Love their Steak, and for those on a budget, maybe the Flank Steak affords them the opportunity to eat steak were they might not otherwise be able to afford the New York Cut Sirloin. London Broil alla the Flank Steak affords them an opportunity at their "Steak Fix" at an reasonable price.

Two things Dude wants you to know about London Broil. One, it has to be cooked at about Medium Rare. If cooked longer, it gets quite tough. At Medium Rare it stays somewhat tender. So if you don't eat Medium Rare meat and like yours cooked Med Well or Well Done, "Forget about having London Broil." It's not for you. Dudes point two, though Flank Steak isn't the tastiest cut in the land, you can fix it up to make it taste even better. Some nice Mushrooms sautéed in butter or a quick pan sauce works wonders.

London Broil can be cooked on a Backyard Grill or as the Dude prefers in a Skillet, aka Frying Pan. Dude do not recommend cooking it under a Household Broiler, this is the "WORST THING" you could ever do, the Dude says. And most people in America do it this. Dude learned from his Mom that cooking the London Broil under the Broiler was no dam good. She cooked it in a pan, that's the way the Dude does, and if you Achievers out there want good results like the Dudes with your London Broil, you'll cook it in a pan. You're results will be infinitely better.

COOKING LONDON BROIL

1 fresh Flank Steak
Kosher or Sea Salt and Ground Black Pepper
2 tablespoons Sweet or Lightly Salted Butter
2 tablespoons vegetable oil (Corn, Canola, Soy)
6 tablespoons of Red or White Wine or water
2 teaspoons Gravy Master or Maggi's

1. Season the Flank Steak with salt & pepper.

2. Heat your Skillet over a high flame for two minutes.
Add 2 Tablespoons vegetable oil to pan.

3. Add the Flank Steak and cook for 3 minutes.

4. Turn the steak over and cook for another 3 minutes
over high heat.

5. Turn the flame down to medium and cook Steak for 2
minutes more on each side. Take steak out of pan and
put on a platter to rest for a few minutes.

6. Put wine or water in pan that you cooked the Steak in.
Scrape bottom of pan to dislodge the brown bits
sticking to pan, there is an abundance of flavor in these
brown bits which will Help Make your delicious sauce).
Add Gravy Master.

7. Let liquid reduce to half its original volume.
8. Turn flame off. Add butter to pan and move Pan in a
circular motion so the butter will mix in with pan juices,
making your tasty sauce.

9. Quickly slice your Flank Steak across the grain which is cutting across the shorter end of the Steak. Slice to about 1/8 of an inch thick.

10. Place meat on everyone's plate with potato and or vegetable of your choice. Spoon sauce of London Broil and Enjoy!

NOTE: You do not have to make the sauce if you think it might be too difficult. If so, you can stop after step 5 and continue to step 10 and the slicing and serving of the London Broil. You can also use your favorite bottled Steak Sauce.

Another way the Dude likes to serve his London Broil or any steak with sauté some sautéed mushrooms. Sauté them in butter with salt & pepper and serve over the London Broil.

Yet another option would be to serve a store bought premade "Gravy" with the London Broil, though Dude personally recommends against this option, if you want to, it wouldn't be any great sin.

And along with the London Broil or any Steak, Dude usually serves his Dads Home-Fries and if in season 2 or 3 slices of nice Beefsteak Tomato's sprinkled with salt.

Serve with; Baked, Boiled, or Mashed Potatoes, and some Green Veg or Buttered Carrots. Whatever?

PORK CHOPS

Pork Chops? Dude just Loves them! They're Cheap, Tasty, Quick and Easy to cook! They're almost as American as Apple Pie. And the Dude says, "What's better than that?" If you Love eating meat, then eating Pork Chops is one of the easiest and Tastiest ways The Dude knows. All you do is season each side with salt & pepper, heat a pan, throw the pork chops in and cook them about 5 or 6 minutes the side, depending on the thickness of the chops. Nothing can be easier Dude says, except a Hard-Boiled Egg.

Dude loves having a couple tasty Pork Chops with Apple Sauce on the side. He's been eating them that way since childhood and doesn't see any reason to stop, or eat them any other way. Yeah Pork Chops with Apple Sauce is American as Apple Pie. "Hey that's the Apple Pie part," the Dude says, "The Apple Sauce?"

Dude says he has his Pork Chops whenever they're on sale at Ralph's or some other joint. Dude wants to give all you Achievers out there some good solid advice that will help you save some extra Cash, and quite a good amount of it during the course of a year. Be smart and do as the Dude does. He doesn't go to the supermarket saying he wants to have some Pork Chops and he goes and buys them and they're like $4.99 a pound or something like that. No Dude goes to the supermarket, sees what's on sale when he's there, and buys just items that are on sale. "The Dude" never pays Full-Retail as Walter and other friends of the Dudes who are of the Jewish faith. It's the "smart" and sensible thing to do. He'll say it again, "Never Pay Full Retail." Are you dumb or something?

Listen to The Dude. Don't buy the Pork Chops at $4.99 a pound. Buy them when they're on Sale for much less. Don't buy chicken at $1.99 a pound or more when you know eventually it will be on sale for anywhere from .79 cents a pound to $1.29 a pound at most.

Follow the Dudes good advice and you might find an extra thousand to $3,000 a year in your pockets. Seriously! More money to buy Kahlua or gasoline for driving around, or a New Bowling Ball, Weed, whatever? Just don't throw it away buying stuff for the higher rather than the lesser price. "It's Money in Your Pockets Man," so says our hero, The Dude. Be smart and follow his advice and good ole "Duder Wisdom."

DUDE STYLE PORK CHOPS

When it comes to Pork Chops, again, The Dude says keep it simple. All you gotta do is season the pork chops with Salt & Pepper, brown them nicely in a pan and serve em with, "You gotta have Apple Sauce" with you Pork Chops the Dude advises. Dude says you should have your Pork Chops with Apple Sauce and you might want to make some Home-Fires or other veggie besides the Apple Sauce. Then again you might not. Open a can of Kernel Corn, heat it up, drain and put on the plate with a knob of butter and you're all set. "Speaking of butter," Dude says, "Spread a little bit of butter on top of the pork chops once they're on the plate, it Yummies them-up! Abide!

INGREDIENTS:
For 2 People. Double up for 4

2 Chops for one person or you might want
3 if you Love them as much as Dude does
4 Center Cut Pork Chops
Salt & Black Pepper
2 tablespoons vegetables oil

PREPARATION:

1. Season the Pork Chops with Salt & Pepper

2. Heat a frying pan that is larger enough to hold 4 Pork Chops to high flame for 2 minutes.
3. Add Pork Chops to pan and cook over high heat for two minutes on each side.

4. Turn heat down to medium and cook Pork Chops for 2 minutes on each side.

5. Remove Pork Chops to plate with Apple Sauce and potato and or vegetables of your choice.

Dudes Ingenious "NO COOK CHICKEN DINNER"

Here's a pretty "Nifty Invention" of The Dude that he calls "The No Cook Chicken Dinner." The no Cook Chicken Dinner? If you have a place close to your house that makes a nice Rotisserie Chicken pick one up. Dude gets his fully cooked Deli roast Chicken at Ralph's.

With one whole chicken you should be able to get two to three meals from it. Spend two dollars on a Cucumber and tomato to make a nice Cucumber & Tomato Salad. Eat a quarter or half the chicken hot with the salad and the next day you can make a tasty chicken sandwich with slices of tomato and cucumber. You can have it again for dinner that night.

Or you can do a favorite of the Dudes. Pick up a Cooked Chicken at Ralph's and have a Sexy Dinner with Maude. You can have one too, with your special someone, or a friend who wants you to Help Her Conceive. As the Dude does, you'll pick up a nice bottle of wine, whatever you like within your means, as low as $5.99 at Trader Joe's or other place where you can get a nice inexpensive bottle of wine. Make the Cucumber Tomato Salad with your favorite bottled salad dressing, burn a couple candles and Let One Thing Lead to Another!

MAUDE'S MEATLOAF

Yeah, Maude likes Meatloaf. She loves it in fact. It's her favorite thing to eat, and she loves whipping one up after a day of painting "Strongly Vaginal Art." Sometimes Maude invites Knox over for dinner, Meatloaf of course, or she might want to coax The Dude into a *Zesty Enterprise*, no Nymphomaniac Stepmothers" allowed. Maude will butter the Dude up with a home-cooked meal of her famous Meatloaf?

Knox loves the Meatloaf and made a very "Artsy Esoteric Video," called "Maude's Meatloaf."

Maude and Knox had a World Premier Screening of the video at a friends Palazzo on The Grand Canal in Venice one year during the Biennale. They watched the video and everyone got very hungry during the screening, and afterwards all the select few special guest (60 people) were treated to a lavish sit-down-dinner of "Maude's Meatloaf." They started the dinner with Crabmeat Salad with Prosecco, moved on to a plate of a Venetian Specialty "Riso Bisi" (Fresh Pea Risotto) that Knox supervised, and for the main course of "Maudy's Famous Meatloaf." The night was a huge success. Maude and Knox talk about it all the time, which Dude always finds quite annoying, Maude's "Friend with The Cleft Asshole." "He-he-he," Knox laughs silly.

Yes, the Dude says that you just gotta have a good Meatloaf recipe in your repertoire. He wanted one, and once he tasted Maude's, he just had to have it. The recipe that is! Dude says this Meatloaf is great for parties. You can mix up all the ingredients, put it into loaf pans, and you just throw it in the oven an hour before your guests arrive.

And the Dude says, if you make extra, two Meatloaves instead of one, they make "Awesome Meatloaf Sandwiches" for the next couple of days or so. And here's some more Dude wisdom. He thinks he told you this already. He can't remember, "A lot of *stuff* rollin around in ole Duder's Head." Remember. Whenever you take some time to cook. Don't just make enough food for that one meal. Well only if you make a quick meal that takes 20 minutes or less. But if you are cooking a meal that takes an hour-and-a-half or more to cook, cook something that reheats well (Soup, Chili, Stews, Meatloaf) and that you can get several meals from, Dude calls this "Time Saving." Just like saving Money and not wasting money. You save time and don't waste it. More time to Bowl and drive-around. Abide in this, more "Duderly Wisdom."

This Meatloaf is great with Mashed or a Baked Potato, or simple boiled, drained, and buttered Carrots. Or you can simply serve a nice green salad along with some Baguette or other type bread.

Once you know the very basic recipe, you can change it up by adding different spices or things like sautéed Mushrooms diced Ham, or Green or Red Bell Peppers, whatever you like.

MAUDE'S MEATLOAF

2 pounds fresh Ground Beef
1 medium Onion, peeled and diced fine
1 Egg
½ cup Seasoned Bread Crumbs
¼ teaspoon Salt & ½ teaspoon Black Pepper
6 Tablespoons Tomato Ketchup

3 Tablespoons chopped Fresh Parsley (Optional)

1. Place all the ingredients in a large mixing bowl. Just put half the ketchup now and reserve the other half to spread over top of Meatloaf later.

2. Mix all the ingredients with your hands until thoroughly mixed.

3. Pre-Heat your oven to 350 degrees.

4. Grease a Loaf Pan with vegetable oil or butter. Place ground beef mixture in loaf-pan and press meat down, then bang the loaf pan a couple times to prevent air spaces.

5. Coat top of Meatloaf with remaining Ketchup.

6. Bake in 350 degree oven for about 1 hour and15 minutes.

7. After about 1 ¼ hours, remove Meatloaf from oven and let cool on counter for about 15 minutes. Remove from pan.

8. Cut Meatloaf into 1 ½ to 2" slices and serve with potato, vegetable or salad.

PS .. Double up this recipe and make two Meatloaf's at the same time and you'll have tasty leftovers for Meatloaf Sandwiches the following two days. Serve the Meatloaf with any of The Dudes Potato recipes, and or any or the Green Vegetables, or buttered Carrots, or whatever you want.

FRUITS and VEGGIES

Did you know that for a while some had wondered and pondered if The Dude was a vegetarian or not. As we know by now, "The Dude Is Not A Vegetarian. The Dude has, does now, and most likely will always eat meat. He grew up with it. Heck, comes from a family of hard-working, Blue Collar Polish Stock. Big Big Big Meat-Eaters! Lot's of Polish Kielbasa, Pork Chops, Ham, and what not. Meat is in the Dudes veins. However, The Dude is a Californian, he lives in LA, and though yes The Dude does love his meat, especially his Chili, the Dude knows that he needs to have a balanced and recommended diet, of eating lots of fresh fruits and vegetable, and every day. Dude in fact goes meat-less at least two or three days a week. He loves his meat, and chicken too, and don't forget about Pork Chops, and his Polish Heritage Kielbasa. Yes, Dude loves his meat. He's not going to be no vegetarian, too restrictive for The Dude. And Dude doesn't like any restriction being put upon him. He eats what he wants. Some days the Dude likes and wants to go Meat-Less, though he loves his Pork Chops and Chili, Dude knows that too much meat is not good for one's health, so when it comes to eating and ole Duder's diet. He does the right things and eats balanced daily meals. But when The Dude feels like a Steak, a Burger, some of Maude's Meatloaf, he's gonna have it, and dammed if anyone's gonna tell him he's not."

CARROTS CABBAGE & GREEN BEANS

Carrots and Green Beans, two of The Dudes favorites , says he especially likes carrots, buttered up, they're good for ole Duder's eyes..

Dude says the carrots are real easy to prepare. Just peel the carrots, slice them, cook them in boiling water for about 6 minutes, drain, then slather on a little butter, season with salt and pepper and you're set. These buttered carrots are great as an accompaniment for just about anything. Dude will put them on a plate with his Pork Chops, they're great with London Broil or a Sirloin Steak, or on the plate with ¼ of Dudes Deli Cooked Chicken from Ralph's.

You can make Green Beans the same way, and to combine both together, Half Carrots and Half Green Beans, you'll double your pleasure. Making these vegetables is a good way to get part of your daily fruit and vegetable fix, and Dudes says, make sure you get your fair share.

GREEN BEANS

For GREEN BEANS, follow the same procedures above, replacing the carrots with Green Beans (String Beans) substituting Sesame Oil for Butter is another option that gives an Asian Flavor.

Dude says, if you want to make Italian-Style Green Beans, sauté the green beans in olive oil and garlic. Peel and thinly slice 3 cloves of garlic. Place 5 tablespoons olive oil in a large sauté pan and turn heat on to medium flame. When garlic starts to brown a little turn heat down to lowest flame. Add a pinch of hot red-pepper-flakes to oil. Cook for 30 seconds, then add green beans that have been blanched in boiling water for 4-5 minutes and drained. Add these beans to pan with garlic and olive oil. Turn heat up to high and sauté 2-3 minutes. Season with salt & black pepper and serve.

COOKING CARROTS

1. To serve two people, peel 2 or three medium sized Carrots.

2. Fill a small pot with water and ½ teaspoon of Salt. Bring water to the boil over a high flame.

3. Boil carrots four to five minutes until they are fork tender. Turn heat off and drain carrots in a colander.
Place a portion of drained carrots on a plate, sprinkle with salt and coat with a little Knob of Butter.

NOTE: If you want just boiled carrots, omit putting on the butter.

BOILED CABBAGE
"KIELBASA TOO?"

Boiled Cabbage? Doesn't sound too appetizing you say. If you think so, you couldn't be more wrong. Boil it, then The Dude slathers on some Butter. Sprinkle on some Salt and Pepper and you've got some-thing quite tasty. Dude says this item is cheap, quick, and easy to make and tasty too. All the qualities The Dude loves in his food. Boiled Cabbage goes really well with just about every-thing, but for some really easy and lightning fast to make, one of The Dudes All-Time-Favorites is Boiled Cabbage with Kielbasa. Hey Dude is Polish man! Of course he loves his Kielbasa. He loves it even more, now as a grown man. For The Dude can go pick up a ring of nice Polish Kielbasa for four or five bucks, get a head of cabbage for another dollar, and he'll be set for four to six tasty meals that are virtually almost no work (very little any way), and it's ready in a flash. Like ten minutes.

lbasa depending on the size of the piece of Kielbasa he cuts for each meal. To make The Dudes Quick and Easy Keilbasa and Cabbage, put a pot of boiling water on the stove. Cut the cabbage in half, then cut off a wedge of cabbage, the size you want for this meal. Put the wedge of cabbage and some salt in the water and let boil for four minutes. Add the kielbasa and continue cooking the two together for 4 minutes. Turn the heat off, and drain the cabbage and Kielbasa in a colander. Place both on a plate. Sprinkle salt and pepper onto the cabbage, and slather on a pat of butter. You now have

Got Any Kahlua?

The Dudes Boiled Cabbage and Kielbasa Dinner, quick and easy, and oh so tasty. Enjoy.

When the Dude has some Kielbasa in the frig, he'll definitely have it for breakfast one or two days, simply by boiling a piece of Kielbasa and scrambling or frying a couple of eggs, and Voila, you got a breakfast fit for a King. A Dude or Achiever like you too.

POTATOES BAKED BOILED & MASHED

Potatoes, an American favorite, for The Dude too. Potatoes, cheap, easy and nourishing. Bake em, boiled, Fried, Sautéed, and Mashed. Yummm!!! Potato Salad too.

MASHED POTATOES

5 large Russet, Maine, or Idaho Potatoes
1/3 cup of Whole Milk, hot.
3 tablespoons Butter
Salt & White Pepper

1. Place a 4 quart pot on stove and fill with water and 1 teaspoon salt.

2. Peel potatoes and cut into for equal pieces.

3. Add potatoes to water and bring back to the boil. Simmer for about 10 to 12 minutes or potatoes are just tender when pierced with a fork.

4. Remove potatoes from heat. Drain potatoes in a colander. Place potatoes back in the pot they cooked in, making sure all water has been drained and pot is dry.

5. Mash potatoes with hand potato masher. Add Butter and mix with a wooden spoon. Add Salt and Pepper to taste. Add the Hot Milk a little at a time, stirring w/ wooden spoon. Serve immediately.

BOILED POTATOES

Boiled Potatoes are Super Easy to make. Wash or Peel them. Through them in salted boiling water. Boil them for a few minutes, drain, and season them with a little Salt and with or without Butter or Olive Oil and Voila, you've got Boiled Potatoes as simple as that. Serve with a Steak, Pork, Chicken, or any Stew. Or cool, slice, and make into Potato Salad. Red New Potatoes are Best for boiling and look great on a plate with skin still on.

8-10 New Potatoes, all about the same size, washed.
Kosher or Sea Salt
Optional: Butter or Olive Oil, chopped fresh, Parsley

1. Cut potatoes in half and place in a pot large enough to hold them. Cover with water, add one teaspoon Salt.

2. Bring water to the boil, then lower to a steady simmer and cook potatoes for about 10 to 14 minutes or until potatoes are tender when pierced with a fork.

3. Drain potatoes in a colander. Place a few on each plate along with whatever protein you are serving. Dress with Butter or Olive Oil and season with Salt to taste.

BAKED POTATOES: Wash do not peel, 1-4 Idaho Potatoes. Bake in a 375 degree oven for 1 hour. They're done. Serve with Steak, London Broil, or Pork Chops.

MUSTARD GREENS & BOK CHOY BABY

Like most Californians the Dude likes his veggies. And The Dude and most Californians love both Mexican and Asian Foods. And when it comes to Asian vegetables, The Dude really loves his Mustard Greens and especially his Baby Bok Choy. Dude really loves Baby Bok Choy and eats it quite a bit for a number of reasons. Number one, is that it's always nice and fresh and the Chinese Grocer is usually selling it 2 pounds for just $1.50 .. The baby Bok Choy is super easy and fast to cook up. And the Dude has a wonderful method a Chinese friend showed him. No it wasn't "Woo." He Peed on the Dudes Fuckin Rug man!

Walter: It really tied the room together, did it not?

Dude: Fucking eh!"

Dude: This China-Man who peed on my Rug, I can't go give him a bill so what the Fuck are you talking about?

Walter: What the Fuck are you talking about? This China-Man is not the issue! I'm talking about drawing a line in the sand, Dude. Across this Line you do not, uh—and also, Dude, China-Man is not the preferred, uh—Asian-American, please.
Dude: Walter this not a guy who built the
          Rail Roads here, this guy who peed on my ..

Walter: What the Fuck are you---

182

Got Any Kahlua?

Dude: Walter he peed on my Rug---

Walter: He Peed on your FUCKING RUG !!!

No it wasn't Woo. The Dude can't stand that Fuckin Guy. "He's not House-Broken." He peed on The Dudes Fuckin Rug!

Anyway, back to the Bok Choy. Baby Bok Choy.

Each one is a lovely little package that looks great on any plate, Dude says. You wash a few under cold running water. Split them in half, in boiling water for just 3 minutes, drain, and season them up with a little Salt, Garlic Red Pepper Sauce and Sesame Oil. Yumm!

Well the Dudes recipe and wonderfully tasty and simple method is below. Follow it. Dude loves serving Baby Bok Choy this way with one or two Fried Eggs or with dry seasoned Ramen Noodles for a fast (less than 7 minutes) and tasty Breakfast or quick meal any old time of the day. The Dude is a Genius! Fuckin Eh!

DUDES BABY BOK CHOY

4 pieces of Baby Bok Choy washed and split in half
Kosher, Sea, or Table Salt
1 tablespoon Sesame Oil
Chinese Garlic Red Pepper Paste or
other Hot Sauce like Sriracha

Cooking Procedures:

1. Fill a small pot with water and 1 teaspoon salt on top of stove and bring to the boil.

2. Add the Baby Bok Choy and cook for about 2-3 minutes. This is blanching. You want to soften up the Bok Choy just a little bit, keeping it firm and crisp and retaining all of its beautiful bright Green Color.

3. Remove from and drain in a wire strainer or colander. Place on plate and season with Salt Sesame Oil and Hot Sauce of your sauce.

Note: If you don't like Hot Sauce, you can use a little Ground Black Pepper instead.

VARIATION: To cook MUSTARD GREENS, follow the exact same steps, replacing Mustard Greens for the Baby Bok Choy, or ANYTHING. And The DUDE says, serve these MUSTARD GREENS or BABY BOK CHOY on a plate with just about anything; Fish, Chicken and even Pork Chops or Steak.

DUDE ON DESSERTS

Yes, The Dude on deserts. Dude rarely cooks desserts, but Once In a Blue Moon he might. Dude doesn't have a lot of desserts in his cooking repertoire. It's enough just to cook the Savory Food. Dude, maybe once every two years will make a Cheesecake or Pumpkin Pie for Thanksgiving.

Dude being the Genius he is and a lover of all things Kahlua has invented a Genius Recipe, that's quite yummy, "It's got Kahlua in It" of course. It's super easy to make and is very versatile. The Dude wants you to learn it. It's The Dudes "Famous Chocolate Kahlua Sauce. You can put it on everything; Ice Cream, Pound Cake, Twinkies, whatever, and for a fun and special treat, you can cut up fresh Bananas, Strawberries and whatever other fruits you like, and use Dudes Chocolate Kahlua Sauce as the base of a Chocolate Fondue. It's Awesome, Fun and quite impressive too. "Do it," Dude says.

DUDES CHOCOLATE KAHLUA SAUCE

¾ Milk, 3/4 cup Heavy Cream
½ cup Sugar
¼ cup Dutch Cocoa powder
6 oz. Dark Chocolate (chopped)
2 tablespoons Butter, ¼ teaspoon Salt
1 teaspoon pure Vanilla extract
8 tablespoons Kahlua

1. Put Heavy Cream, Milk, and sugar in a medium size stainless- steel pot. Bring up to the boil. Lower flame to very low heat.

2. Add Cocoa and salt and heat while stirring over low flame for 3 minutes. Turn heat off.

3. Add dark chocolate and butter. Mix until chocolate and butter have melted and have blended into a nice smooth consistency.

4. Add Kahlua and Vanilla and mix to incorporate.

This is Delicious and taste great poured over a variety of different things. Dude likes to pour it over Vanilla Ice Cream. And other desserts and to frost Cakes or Cupacakes with. For a nice tasty desert that is quick and easy, Dude picks up some nice Pound Cake at Ralph's. They often have a really good one for just $1.49 .. Dude slices off a piece of Pound Cake and toast it in a frying pan with a bit of butter, then pours on the Hot Fudge Sauce. It's Kahlua-y Fudgy Good!

TWINKIES??? Dudes Chocolate Covered

How To Make Em !!!

You got Twinkies? You Got the Kahlua Sauce! Guess What? Dudes Chocolate Kahlua Twinkies are the one and only logical step. Abide!

1. Get a Box of Twinkies.

2. Make the above Recipe for Dudes Chocolate Kahlua Sauce.

3. Get a wire cooking rack and place over a cookie pan (this is to catch all the Tasty Sauce that drips down).

4. Place Twinkies on wire-cooking rack. Evenly pour your Dudes Chocolate Kahlua Sauce over the Twinkies. Some of the sauce will drip down on to pan. Save it!

5. Let cool at room temperature for 10 minutes. Place Chocolate Kahlua Covered Twinkies in the refrigerator for 12 minutes to cool.

6. Serve Chocolate Kahlua-Covered-Twinkies as is, or accompanied with a Caucasian (White Russian). And Abide!

WHITE RUSSIAN CUPCAKES

White Russians Cupcakes? No Dude doesn't make them. There're Maudy's little invention. Even though she doesn't live with The Dude, she likes him quite a bit. Heck, he helped her conceive. So Maude felt like showing a little gratitude. Knowing how much Jeffrey (as Maude calls him) loves his Kahlua, Maude created this in honor of his Dudeness, Jeffrey Lebowski," a.k.a. *The Dude*. "They're right tasty," as The Cowboy Stranger would say, and quite easy to make. Enjoy em!

INGREDIENTS:

1 cup Sugar
½ cup Butter
2 Eggs
2 teaspoons Vanilla Extract
1 ½ cups All-Purpose Flour
1 ¾ teaspoons Baking Powder
½ cup Milk
3 tablespoons Kahlua

1. Preheat oven to 350 degrees.

2. In a mixing bowl, cream together the Butter & Sugar.

3. Beat the eggs, one at a time, then stir in the Vanilla.

4. Combine Flour & Baking Powder in a separate small bow, then add to Creamed sugar and mix well.

5. Add Milk, and stir until smooth.

6. Place paper cupcake-liners and place in cupcake Baking Pan. Spoon cupcake batter into the cupcake liners. Bake for at 350 degrees for about 16-18 minutes, until a toothpick that is poked into the center of a cupcake comes out clean.

7. Take cupcakes out of oven and set aside to cool.

8. Brush tops of cupcakes with Kahlua. Let it soak into the cake.

KAHLUA FROSTING

8 ounces Cream Cheese, at room temperature
1 stick Butter, room temperature
3 cups Powdered Sugar
½ cup Cocoa, unsweetened
½ teaspoon Pure Vanilla Extract
6 tablespoons Kahlua
3 tablespoons Heavy Cream

1. Beat cream cheese, sugar, and butter together until smooth and thoroughly mixed.

2. Add Cocoa and mix. Add Vanilla and Kahlua and mix. Add Heavy Cream, and mix till smooth.

3. Frost each cupcake with frosting.

NEW YORK CHEESECAKE

Dude ripped this recipe out of a woman's magazine when he was waiting at the Doctor's Office in the waiting-room that Maude sent him to. "That Sly Little Devil Maude, Naughty, Naughty." Dude says it's a darn good recipe.

INGREDIENTS:

6 ounces Graham Crackers
1 tablespoon Sugar
4 tablespoons Sweet Butter, melted
3 pounds Cream Cheese at room temperature
1 pound Sour Cream
2 cups Granulated Sugar
7 large Eggs
1/8 teaspoon Salt
1 teaspoon Pure Vanilla Extract

1. If you have a Food Processor and want to Make a Graham Cracker Crust, Great! Otherwise you can skip making the cake with this crust and just spread some soft butter on a 10 inch Spring Form Pan.

2. If making a Graham Cracker Crust, place the crackers and sugar in food processor and process until the Graham Crackers have completely turned to crumbs. Place the crumbled Graham Crackers in large mixing bowl, add melted butter and mix with a fork or wooden spoon.

3. Spread soft butter on the insides of a 10" Spring-Form pan. Put the graham crackers into this pan. Spread these crumbs evenly into bottom of pan with hands.

4. Place Cream Cheese, Sour Cream, and Sugar in a large mixing bowl. Mix with an electric hand Held mixer, softening the Cream Cheese.

5. Add eggs, two at a time until all are mixed in. Add salt and vanilla, mix for 30 seconds.

6. Pour Cheese mixture into Spring Pan over the Graham Cracker Crust.

7. Bake Cheesecake in a 325 degree oven for 1 ¼ hours, or until a toothpick that is stuck into the middle of the Cheesecake comes out clean, with nothing sticking on it.

8. Remove from oven and let cool to room temperature for about an hour.

9. Place Cheesecake in refrigerator and let cool in refrigerator for at least 2 ½ hours before serving.

Note: If you feel like Gilding-The-Lilly a bit. Slather on some of The Dudes Famous Chocolate Kahlua Sauce when serving the Cheesecake. Wow, that's Abiding.

"The Dude Abides! I don't know about you, but I take comfort in that. It's good knowin he's out there. The Dude. Takin' er easy for all us sinners. Shoosh. I sure hope he makes the finals."

The Cowboy Stranger

IN CLOSING

\Well, hope all you fellow Achievers out there enjoyed the book. We sure enjoyed putting it together, "Lot's of *Ins*, a lot of *Outs*, a lot of *what-have-youz* (recipes), a lot of strands to keep in Dudes head man. Lots of strands in old Duder's head."

Before all this, before "Certain Things Came to Light, Man. Certain information, New Shit (The Dudes collected recipes), many have pondered and thought about what The Dude ate, was he vegetarian or not? Well, "Not!" Dude can't have those kind of restrictions, Man! He didn't eat anything in the movie. Well no two-hour movie can ever fit everything in that needs to be said, shown. Heck, The Dude never actually Bowled in the movie either. Yes it's true. You didn't realize that? He stands there talking to Walter and Donny, Bowling Ball in hand, "That's Fucking interesting man," but he never throws the Bowling Ball down the lane. You never see the Dude bowl. Does that mean he doesn't Bowl? "Not!" Same thing with the In-N-Out Burgers. Just because you don't see the Dude eating one in the car, it doesn't mean he doesn't eat them. Doesn't mean he didn't eat his before, and is already finished as Donny and Walter still munch on theirs. "He's driving Man!"

Did the Dude subsist on Beer, Bar Peanuts, and White Russians (Caucasians Gary) alone? Hell no!

And The Dude sure was a Lazy Man, possibly the laziest Man in all of Los Angeles County, which would put him in competition for "Laziest World Wide." Would a man like this cook his own meals? Hell yeah, he has to. As we've already stated, the guy doesn't work, he's on *Unemployment*. Yes the Dude was a lazy man, but lazy for work, and not having a job to go to. The Dude has lots of free time on his hands in-between Bowling, Tai Chi, driving around, a-little-bit-of-this-a-little-bit-of-that, drinking White Russians, and Coffee. The Dude has got plenty of free time and time to cook. The Dude is unemployed. He gets unemployment checks (not substantial) and they can only go so far. Yes, Dude has to pay the Rent to Monti, get gas for the car, pay bowling fees, and keep himself in Kahlua and Weed. Not cheap items either. Dude could buy some other Cheap Coffee Liqueur at half the price, but that would never do, it's not Kahlua Man! Dude needs to buy everything he requires with that unemployment check, stretch every Dollar as far as it'll go. He's gotta be smart, he's gotta be thrifty. He's gotta cook, "Gotta Feed The Monkey!" That's all there is to it. Eating out or ordering take-out often would be far too expensive! The Dude would never have the money to buy Kahlua and "What Not." Out of necessity, The Dude has to cook a lot of his meals. Doesn't mean that he can't stop at The Taco Stand for a taco or two here-and-there, or that he can't have a In-N-Out Double-Double every now and then. No, he can occasionally order-in or eat; a Taco, Burger, or Chili Dog out, but he needs to get most of his meals at home. It's a lot cheaper, and with the money he saves he can buy??? Well you know? Besides all this, the Dude needs to cook, and it's not just that, The Dude likes it. Yes The Dude enjoys Cooking, it relaxes him. It's Zen Man! And The Dude Abides in that. Cooking!

So my dear friends, we do hope you like this little thing we have put together and hope it sheds some new light. Yes certain things have come to light. "Certain information, New Shit Man."

We hope you enjoy, re-enact, and Eat as the Dude does. Try as many recipes as you can, Cook, Eat, relax (while listening to Creedence as your Chili simmers away). You'll *save* a good lot of *Money*. Yes, if you follow these recipes and methods "set down" you will save a good lot of Money, and time too. All the Dudes cooking methods and recipes have been accumulated by The Dude and are designed as a whole complete method for the enjoyment of cooking and eating, *saving time, and Money*. Poor ole Dude "Never got that 20 Grand Man!" The guy needs a new car, a second-hand new car that is.

So, read. You've already done that. But no, not just once, this book is a reference you'll use over-and-over-again, year-after-year. Gotta refer to the recipes and advice man! And every time you do, you'll think of The Dude, you'll feel him, his great "Duderly Vibe," his presence, and …

So continue reading, show your friends, the family, fellow Achievers, and you know, always Abide!

By The Same Author

La TAVOLA

SUNDAY SAUCE
"When Italian-Americans Cook"
1 AMAZON BEST SELLER LIST

THE FEAST of THE 7 FISH
"Italian Christmas"

Printed in Great Britain
by Amazon.co.uk, Ltd.,
Marston Gate.